Introduction to Electricity Supply and Regulation in India

By Siva Prasad Bose

Published by Joy Bose

Copyright © 2022 Siva Prasad Bose

All rights reserved. No part of this book may be reproduced in any form on by an electronic or mechanical means, including information storage and retrieval systems, without permission in writing from the publisher.

Contents

Dedication

Preface

Acknowledgements

Chapter 1: Terms and Concepts Related to Electricity Generation and Transmission

Chapter 2: Electrical Power Generation

Chapter 3: Electrical Power Transmission

Chapter 4: Electric Distribution System

Chapter 5: Electric Power Substation

Chapter 6: Electric Energy Measurement

Chapter 7: Electric Protective Devices

Chapter 8: History of Electricity Supply Legislation in India

Chapter 9: Electricity Act 2003

Chapter 10: National Tariff Policy

Chapter 11: Regulatory Framework

Chapter 12: Regulation of Electricity Transmission, Distribution and Trading

Chapter 13: Some Considerations for Setting Electricity Tariffs

Chapter 14: Understanding Electricity Tariff Structures in India

Chapter 15: Privatisation of DISCOMs in India

Chapter 16: Smart Grid and Digital Metering

Chapter 17: Sustainability and Renewable Integration

Chapter 18: Future Trends and Emerging Policies

Chapter 19: Conclusion

About the Author

Other Books by Siva Prasad Bose

Dedication

This book is dedicated to all consumers of electricity in India.

Preface

Electricity is the backbone of modern development, and understanding its journey—from generation to consumption, and from policy to pricing—is essential for anyone engaging with India's infrastructure or governance landscape. This book offers an introductory overview of the technical and regulatory aspects of electricity supply in India, written in a concise and accessible format for students, professionals, and interested readers.

The book is divided into two parts. The first part covers the technical dimensions of the electricity sector—generation, transmission, distribution, energy measurement, substations, and smart grids. It also introduces readers to protective devices and smart metering, offering a practical grounding in how electricity physically reaches consumers.

The second part explores the legal and regulatory framework that governs the electricity supply in India. It covers the evolution of legislation from the colonial era to the Electricity Act of 2003, along with discussions on national tariff policy, the roles of regulatory commissions, privatisation of distribution companies (DISCOMs), and sustainability initiatives. Special attention is paid to tariff structures, state-wise differences, and future reforms shaping the sector.

Through this dual focus, the book aims to build both a conceptual and practical understanding of how electricity is managed, priced, and delivered in India. It is our hope that readers will find this volume a useful starting point for deeper exploration, research, and engagement with India's dynamic power sector. This edition has been updated to reflect significant recent developments, including India's achievement of 500 GW of installed power generation capacity in 2025, the landmark milestone of 50% non-fossil fuel electricity capacity five years ahead of target, the Revamped Distribution Sector Scheme (RDSS) and its impact on DISCOM financial health, the Electricity (Amendment) Bill 2022 and its proposed reforms, the PM Surya Ghar: Muft Bijli Yojana for rooftop solar, the National Green Hydrogen Mission, and the growing role of Battery Energy Storage Systems (BESS) in enabling renewable integration.

Acknowledgements

The following books on energy utilization have been consulted for the preparation of the manuscript and are thankfully acknowledged:

- McGraw Hill Concise Encyclopedia of Science and Technology, Sybil P Parker, Editor in Chief
- Energy Technology: Sources of Power, Anthony E Schwaller, St. Cloud State University
- Energy, AK Bakshi, National Book Trust India
- Practical Photovoltaics by Richard J Kemp
- Newnes Electrical Pocket Book, EA Reeves
- Electrical Guide, Srikant BK Lambete, Electrical Consultant
- Thesaurus of Physics, Barnes and Noble
- Uttar Pradesh State Electricity Board: Rate Schedule

- Uttar Pradesh State Electricity Board: Conditions of supply
- Uttar Pradesh State Electricity Board: Summary of Tariff Rationalization Committee Report

Chapter 1: Terms and Concepts Related to Electricity Generation and Transmission

In this chapter we discuss a few basic terms and concepts related to electricity generation and transmission.

1.1 Electric Current

Electric current is the net transfer of electric charge per unit time. It is usually measured in amperes. The passage of electric current involves a transfer of energy, since the current always heats the medium through which it passes, except in the case of superconductivity. Most metals, electrolyte solutions and highly ionized gases are conductors. (Mc Graw Hill Concise Encyclopaedia of Science and Technology, 5th Ed.)

1.2 Frequency (wave motion)

Frequency, in context of wave motion is the number of times which sound pressure, electrical intensity, or other quantities specifying the wave vary from their equilibrium value through a complete cycle in that time.

The most common unit of frequency is the Hertz (Hz). 1 Hz is equal to one cycle per second.

In one cycle there is a positive variation from the equilibrium, a return to equilibrium, then a negative variation, and return to equilibrium. This relationship is often described in terms of the sine wave, and the frequency referred to is that of an equivalent sine wave variation in the parameter under discussion.

1.3 Frequency measurement

Measurement of the frequency of a periodic quantity is defined as the number of times a cyclic phenomenon occurs per unit of time. The second is the commonly used unit of time. Conversely, time may be measured by observing the number of cycles occurring at constant frequency. The ordinary pendulum and household electric clocks are common examples of such time measuring devices.

The only primary frequency standards acceptable for use in the national standards laboratories for frequency reference are atomic standards of the caesium-beam type. Caesium-beam atomic clocks have superseded other types of primary frequency standards, as a consequence of the adoption of the atomic standard as the unit of time.

1.4 Electric Power Measurement

Electric power measurement is the measurement of the time rate at which work is done or energy is dissipated in an electric system.

The work done in moving an electric charge is proportional to the charge and the voltage drop through which it moves. Charge per unit time defines electric current.

Electric power (p) is defined as the product of the current in an electric circuit (i) and the voltage (v) across its terminals in a given time.

$p = i * v$

Another definition of power is given by Ohm's law:

$p = i^2 * R$ where R is the resistance of the circuit.

1.5 Alternating current (AC) and Direct Current (DC)

Alternating current or AC is one in which the current switches its directions periodically, represented as a sign wave. Direct current or DC is one that moves steadily in a fixed direction. Most transmission lines in power systems are AC, since the power loss in transmission is less in AC compared to DC transmission lines.

1.6 Electric Power System

An electric power system is a complex assemblage of equipment and circuits for generating, transmitting, transforming and distributing electrical energy.

Electricity in the large quantities required to supply electric power systems is produced in generating stations, commonly called power plants. Such generating stations should be considered as conversion facilities in which heat energy or fuel such as coal, oil, gas or uranium, or the hydraulic energy of falling water, or the energy of sunlight, is converted to electricity.

The transmission system carries electric power efficiently and in large amounts from the generating stations to consumption areas. Such transmission is also used to interconnect adjacent power systems for mutual assistance in case of emergency and to gain economics for regional operation for the interconnected systems.

A relatively new approach to high voltage long distance transmission is high voltage direct current (HVDC) which has the advantages of less costly lines, lower transmission losses, and none of the system problems that affect the alternating current (AC) systems. However has the disadvantage of needing costly equipment to convert sending end power to direct current (DC) and converting the receiving end DC back to AC.

1.7 Conclusion

In this chapter we have gone through some terms and concepts in the area of electricity power systems.

Chapter 2: Electrical Power Generation

In this chapter, we discuss some mechanisms for the generation of electricity.

2.1 Indian power sector

India is the third highest producer of electricity in the world. As of October 2025, India's total installed generation capacity has surpassed 500 GW — reaching 5,05,023 MW — comprising approximately 245,600 MW of fossil-fuel sources and 259,423 MW of non-fossil fuel sources (including 250,643 MW from renewable energy sources). In a historic milestone achieved in June 2025, India crossed 50% of its installed electricity capacity from non-fossil fuel sources, five years ahead of the target set under its Nationally Determined Contributions (NDCs) to the Paris Agreement. Solar capacity alone crossed 100 GW in January 2025 and reached 132 GW by November 2025. Fossil fuels, mainly coal, continue to provide a significant portion of total electricity generation, though the share of coal in the generation mix has been declining. India has the capacity to produce more power than it needs, although the distribution and transmission systems need to be improved.

Most of the electric power is produced in power plants, also called power stations or generating stations, that are connected to an electrical grid.

2.2 Introduction to Power Plants

Power plants are a means for converting stored energy or potential energy into work. Stationery power plants such as electric generating stations are located near sources of stored energy, such as coal fields or river dams, or are located near the places where the work is to be performed, such as in cities or industrial sites.

Mobile power plants for transportation service are located in vehicles, such as the gasoline engines in automobiles and diesel locomotives for railroads.

Most power plants convert part of the stored energy of fossil fuels into the kinetic energy of a spinning shaft. Some power plants harness nuclear energy. Elevated water supply or run of the river energy is used in hydro electric power plants. Other sources of energy, such as winds, tides, waves, geothermal sources, ocean thermal, nuclear fusion and solar radiation have been of negligible commercial significance in the generation of power despite the magnitudes.

2.2 Electric Power Generation

The production of bulk electrical power for industrial, residential and rural use is known as electric power generation.

Although limited amounts of electricity can be generated by many means including chemical reactions (as in batteries) and engine driven generators (as in automobiles and airplanes) electric power generation generally implies large scale production of electrical power in stationary plants designed for the purpose.

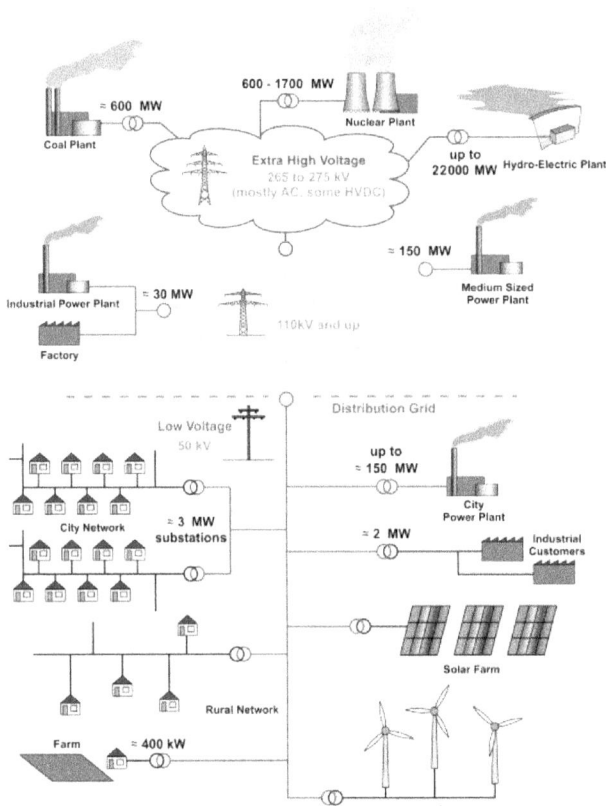

Figure: Layout of an electricity grid. MBizon, CC BY 3.0 <https://creativecommons.org/licenses/by/3.0>, via Wikimedia Commons

The generating unit in these plants converts energy from falling water, coal, natural gas, oil and nuclear fuels to electric energy. Most electric generators are driven either by hydraulic turbines, for conversion of falling water energy, or by steam or gas turbines, for conversion of fuel energy. Limited use is being made of geothermal energy, and work is progressing towards the use of solar energy in various forms. Electrical power generating plants are normally interconnected by a transmission and distribution system to serve the electrical loads in a given area or region.

An electric load is the power requirement of any device or equipment that converts electric energy into light, heat or mechanical energy or otherwise consumes electrical energy as in aluminium reduction or the power requirement of electronic or control devices. The total load on any system is seldom constant. Rather, it varies widely with hourly, weekly, monthly or annual changes in the requirement of the area served. The minimum system load for a given period is termed the base load or the unity load factor component. Maximum loads, usually resulting from temporary conditions are called peak loads. Electrical energy cannot feasibly be stored in large quantities, therefore the operation of the generating plants must be closely coordinated with fluctuations in the load.

Generating plants, often called generating stations, contain apparatus that convert some form of energy to electric energy in bulk. Some important types of generating plants are fossil fuel electric, hydro electric and nuclear electric.

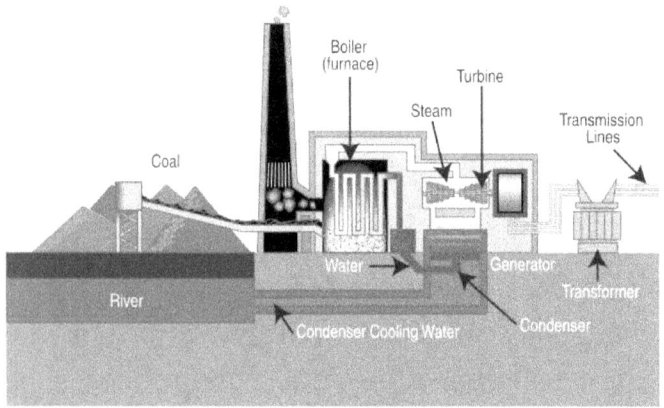

Figure: Coal-fired power station diagram. Tennessee Valley Authority, Public domain, via Wikimedia Commons

The size or capacity of electric utility generating units vary widely depending on the type of unit and duty required, i.e. base, intermediate or peak load service, system size and degree of interconnection with neighbouring systems. Base load units, such as nuclear and some coal fired units, may not be able to change their power output quickly or easily. Intermediate load units, such as some coal, oil or gas fuelled steam generators, are typically of 200 to 600 MW capacity. Peak load units include combustion turbines or hydro electric power stations, and range from tens of megawatts in combustion turbines to hundreds of megawatts (up to 700 MW) in hydroelectric units.

The total installed generating capacity of a system is typically 20% to 30% greater than the annual predicted peak load, in order to provide reserves for maintenance and contingencies.

2.3 Fossil fuel power generation

The fossil fuel electric plant utilises the energy of combustion from coal, oil or natural gas. A typical large plant consists of the following:

- Fuel processing and handling facilities
- A combustion furnace and boiler to produce and superheat the steam
- A steam turbine
- An alternator

- Equipment for plant protection and for control of voltage, frequency and power flows.

A steam plant can frequently be built near a convenient load centre, provided an adequate supply of cooling water and fuel is available, and is usually adaptable to base loading and peak or intermediate loading.

2.4 Coal power generation

In coal power plants, coal is used in a heat engine to produce thermal energy via combustion, which is then converted to mechanical energy typically through steam turbines, which is finally converted to electrical energy via generators.

In many countries including India, the bulk of power generation is done at high efficiency coal fired steam plants, the turbo alternator sets generating power at 11 KV and with ratings around 120 MW but which can go higher in bigger power stations up to 200 MW, 300 MW and 550 MW units.

In a coal powered generator, steam in delivered to the turbine stop valve at pressures higher than 1000 psi and 1050 degrees Fahrenheit. Even greater pressures up to 5000 psi are being used or contemplated and temperatures up to 1200 degrees Fahrenheit are also employed. However, these higher temperatures associated with the higher pressures require special types of austenitic (high strength) steels and many engineering problems yet need to be addressed.

2.5 Diesel electric generation

The principle of diesel power generation is similar to coal, except that diesel is used as the fuel to run the heat engines via combustion.

Diesel electric generation has been used in some power stations but are limited to small outputs. They have the advantage of being lightweight and mobile, enabling them to be used in mobile power stations to be transported to areas where power supply has failed.

Pulverized fuel-fired boilers are used at many generating stations, although they are being increasingly replaced with oil fired boilers since oil is comparatively cheaper.

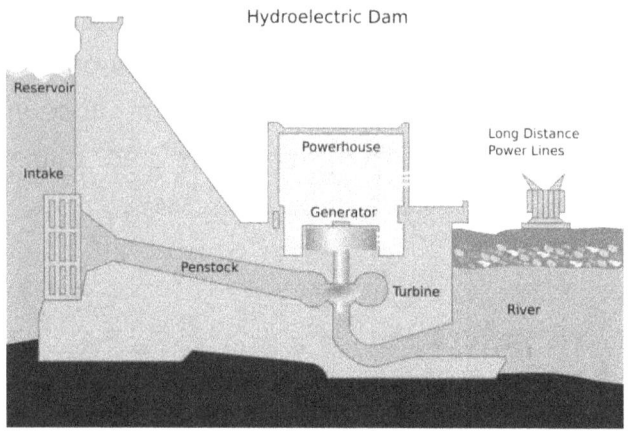

Figure: Cross-section of a hydroelectric dam. By Tennessee Valley Authority; SVG version by Tomia, CC BY-SA 3.0 <http://creativecommons.org/licenses/by-sa/3.0/>, via Wikimedia Commons

2.6 Hydro-electric power

Electricity produced from water is known as hydroelectric power.

The principal behind most conventional hydroelectric power plants is conversion of the potential energy of a dammed river into electrical energy by driving a water turbine that powers a generator. The hydroelectric plant utilizes the potential energy released by the weight of water falling through a vertical distance called head.

The hydroelectric power plant consists of the following components:

- A dam to store the water in a forebay and create part or all of the head
- A penstock to deliver the falling water to the turbine
- A hydraulic turbine to convert the hydraulic energy released to mechanical energy
- An alternating current generator (alternator) to convert the mechanical energy to electrical energy
- Accessory equipment needed to control the power flow, voltage and frequency and to afford the potential required.

Pumped storage hydroelectric plants are being increasingly used. Under suitable geographical and geological conditions, electric energy can, in effect, be stored by pumping water from a low to higher elevation and subsequently releasing this water to the lower elevation through hydraulic turbines. These turbines and their associated generators are reversible. The generators, operating in reverse direction as motors, drive their turbines as pumps to elevate the water. When the water is released through the turbines, electric power is produced by the generators.

In India, hydroelectricity contributes approximately 47,000 MW (around 46 GW) of installed capacity. Major hydroelectric power plants include Koyna hydroelectric project on the Koyna river in Maharashtra, Tehri Dam in Uttarakhand, Bhakra Nangal Dam on Sutlej river in Himachal Pradesh, Srisailam on the Krishna river in Andhra Pradesh and Sardar Sarovar Dam in Gujarat. The government is also promoting pumped storage hydropower projects as a form of grid-scale energy storage to complement variable renewable energy sources; as of 2025, ten pumped storage projects totalling 11,870 MW are under construction across the country.

2.7 Nuclear energy

The use of nuclear energy within our technological society is not new. The process of nuclear energy was first demonstrated by Ernst Rutherford in 1919 when he bombarded nitrogen with alpha particles to cause a nuclear reaction. Earlier, in 1808, atomic theory really developed its first foundations, when John Dalton published a book in which he discussed atoms in detail.

In 1942, Enrico Fermi along with colleagues constructed the first atomic pile which operated on a self-sustaining basis and produced a half watt of power. Soon this pile was allowed to generate 200 watts of power and thus the nuclear age had truly begun. From this point on, a great deal of nuclear energy technology developed. ideas such as atomic structure, atomic numbers, isotopes and energy were further investigated. Many scientific developments followed within a few years of Fermi's discovery.

With the advent of nuclear power and shortage of coal, an ambitious nuclear power programme was embarked upon aimed at building 12 nuclear power stations having a combined output of 500 MW or more.

Figure: Kudankulam Nuclear Power Plant in Tamil Nadu, India, with installed capacity of 2,000 MW. Reetesh Chaurasia, CC BY-SA 4.0 <https://creativecommons.org/licenses/by-sa/4.0>, via Wikimedia Commons

2.8 Nuclear Electric Power Plant

Power derived from fission or fusion nuclear reactions is known as nuclear power. More conventionally, nuclear power is interpreted as the utilization of fission reactions in a nuclear power reactor to produce steam for electrical power production, for ship propulsion or for process heat.

Fission reactions involve the breakup of the nucleus of heavyweight atoms and yield-energy release which is more than a million-fold greater than chemical reactions involving the burning of fuel. Successful control of the nuclear fission reaction provides for the utilization of this intensive source of energy, and with the availability of ample sources of uranium deposits, significantly cheaper fuel costs for electrical power generation are obtainable. Safe, clean and economic nuclear plants have been the objective of the industry's research for a while. On the other hand, critics of nuclear power demand a ban or at least a moratorium on new nuclear plants.

The components of the nuclear/ atomic electric power plant are as follows:

- Nuclear reactor: one or more of the nuclear fuels are utilized in a suitable type of nuclear reactor. This takes the place of the combustion furnace in a typical steam electric plant based on coal or diesel.

- Heat exchanges and boilers, if not combined in the nuclear reactor

- Turbines

- Alternate current generators
- Controls, accessories and auxiliaries

The inherent danger associated with nuclear power, which involves unprecedented quantities of radioactive materials, including possible wide scale use of plutonium, have been recognized. An extensive program for safety, ecological and biomedical studies, research and testing have been integrated with the advancement of the engineering of nuclear power.

2.9 Nuclear Pumped storage schemes

Pumped storage schemes are becoming more important as base load units for nuclear power stations. This means that when the demand for electricity is low, such as during the night-time, the nuclear power station generation will be used to pump water from a lower level up to a reservoir for hydroelectric power generation during the day. Such combined systems with nuclear power pumped storage schemes are used in many cities internationally.

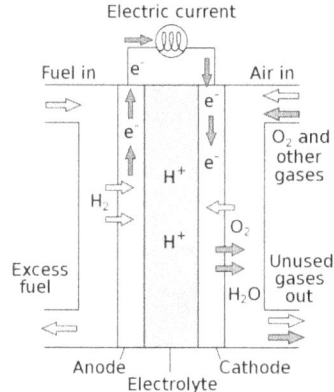

Figure: Scheme of a proton-conducting fuel cell. R.Dervisoglu, Public domain, via Wikimedia Commons

2.10 Fuel cell

A promising development in the field of power generation is the fuel cell and has been a subject of great interest. Here, electricity is generated directly from a chemical reaction. A fuel cell is an energy converter that converts chemical energy of a fuel directly into electrical energy in a continuous process. Though it was discovered over a century ago, it is the target of renewed interest because of the need to find new energy sources.

The efficiency of a fuel cell conversion of chemical energy to electrical can be much greater than that obtained by thermal power conversion, where heat is produced from the chemical reaction by combustion and then transformed partly into mechanical energy by a heat engine, which drives a generator to produce electrical energy. Further energy loss is involved if the direct current generated is converted into an alternating current or AC.

2.11 Fuel cell Reaction

Although in principle the nature of the reactants is not limited, the fuel cell reaction almost always involves a combination of hydrogen with oxygen. If the reaction is harnessed in a galvanic cell working at 100% efficiency, a cell voltage of 1.23 volts results. Fuel cells are of 200-500 Watts capacity and 50-100 mA/cm² current density. Larger prototypes have been produced.

In the present state of development, it is difficult to make a classification of the fuel cell types. The most successful type remains the H_2 - O_2 fuel cell of the direct or indirect type. In the direct type, hydrogen and oxygen are used as such, the fuel being produced in independent installations. The indirect type employs a hydrogen generating unit, which can be used as a raw material in a wide variety of fuel.

2.12 Chemical to electrical conversion - Fuel cell

Many exotic energy converters are being studied today, but one that is affecting a great deal of attention is the fuel cell. A fuel cell is an energy converter that changes chemical energy into electrical energy. Known for over a hundred years, the fuel cell has recently been revived due to a need to develop new energy technology. Due to the energy issue facing our society today, the fuel cell may truly be a significant part of the energy technology in the future.

Figure: Bhadla Solar Park, Rajasthan with a capacity of 2245 MW. Contains modified Copernicus Sentinel data 2020, Attribution, via Wikimedia Commons

2.13 Solar power

The principle behind solar power is the conversion of solar energy from the sun into electricity using photovoltaic cells, which are made of semiconducting materials that use the photovoltaic effect to convert light into an electric current.

Since India is a tropical country with plenty of sunlight, solar power is a fast-growing sector in India. In 2022 the solar installed capacity in India was 53.997 GW. Rooftop solar panel installations have been increasing in different states. Solar power generation facilities include the Bhadla solar park in Rajasthan, which is the world's biggest solar park in terms of generation.

2.14 Conclusion

In this chapter we have briefly gone through different sources of electric power and how it is generated in power plants using different means such as coal, oil, nuclear and water power.

References

Wikipedia. Electricity Sector in India. https://en.wikipedia.org/wiki/Electricity_sector_in_India

Chapter 3: Electrical Power Transmission

In this chapter, we discuss some aspects of transmission of electricity from the power generating stations to the consumers via power transmission lines.

Figure: Electricity Power Transmission lines. Photo by Pixabay from Pexels: https://www.pexels.com/photo/cable-clouds-current-electricity-414967/

3.1 Transmission lines

Transmission lines are a system of conductors, typically cables, suitable for conducting electric power of signals along large distances between two or more receiver terminals with minimal losses and distortions.

Some examples of transmission lines are as follows:

- Commercial frequency electric power transmission lines connect electric generating plants, substations, and their loads.

- Telephone transmissions interconnect telephone subscribers and telephone exchanges.

- Radio frequency transmission lines transmit high frequency electric signals between antennas and transmitters or receivers.

Although only a short cord is needed to connect an electric lamp to a wall outlet, the cord is properly speaking a transmission line. However, in the electrical industry, the term transmission line is only used when both voltages and current at one line terminus may differ appreciably from those at the other terminus.

Transmission lines are described as follows:

- **Electrically short**: if the difference between terminal conditions is attributable simply to the effects of a shunt leakage resistance and capacitance, or to both.
- **Electrically long**: when the properties of the line result from travelling wave phenomenon.

Depending on the configuration and number of conductors and the electric and magnetic fields about the conductors, transmission lines are described as **open wire transmission lines**, **coaxial transmission lines**, **cables or wave guide transmission lines**.

Most transmission lines are overhead or above the ground. For aesthetic reasons, some residential developments have underground distribution systems.

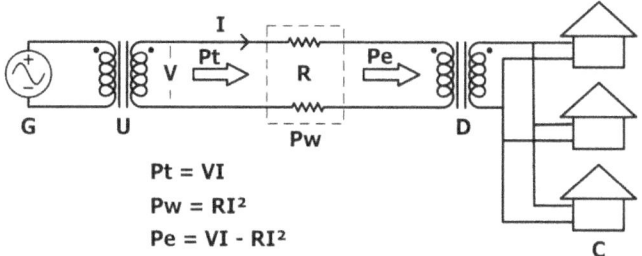

Figure: A schematic representation of long distance electric power transmission. From left to right: G=generator, U=step up transformer, V=voltage at beginning of transmission line, Pt=power entering transmission line, I=current in wires, R=total resistance in wires, Pw=power lost in transmission line, Pe=power reaching the end of the transmission line, D=step down transformer, C=consumers. Roy McCammon, CC0, via Wikimedia Commons

3.2 Theory of transmission lines

When electric power is applied at the terminus of a transmission line, electromagnetic waves are launched and guided along the line. The steady state and transient electrical properties of transmission lines result from the superposition of such waves, termed **direct waves**, and the **reflected waves** which may appear at line discontinuities or at load terminals.

In a uniform or non-tapered transmission line, the voltage or current applied at a sending terminal determines the shape of the initial voltage of current wave. In a line with negligible losses, the transmitted shape remains unchanged. When losses are present, the shape of the voltage or current, unless sinusoidal, is altered, because the phase velocity and alternation vary with the frequency.

3.3 Power Lines

In an electric power system, the facility used to transfer large amounts of power from one location to a distant location is termed a power transmission line.

Techniques of power transmission are presented as follows:

- Power transmission lines are distinguished from sub-transmission and distribution lines by their higher voltages, greater power capabilities and greater lengths.

- With the exception of a few high voltage DC lines for satisfying special requirements, power transmission lines employ three phase alternating currents.

- Such lines require three conductors. The standard frequency is 60 Hz/ 50 Hz. For transmitting large amounts of power over long distances, high voltages are necessary.

- Standard transmission voltages are 69, 115, 138, 161, 230, 345, 500 and 765 KV. These figures refer to the nominal effective voltages between any two of the three conductors.

- The line conductors are usually placed overhead, supported by poles or towers, however they may form part of an underground or underwater cable.

3.4 High Voltage Transmission and the Economics of Electricity Delivery

The use of high voltage in transmission is not merely a technical preference but an economically critical decision. For a given quantity of power transferred, increasing the voltage reduces the current proportionally. Since resistive losses in conductors are proportional to the square of current (expressed as I^2R losses), even a modest increase in transmission voltage produces a dramatic reduction in energy lost as heat along the line. This is why transmission voltages in India range from 132 kV to 765 kV and above for long-distance bulk transfer — the investment in higher-voltage infrastructure is directly offset by savings in transmission losses.

This physical principle has direct consequences for tariff design. Higher voltage connections supply electricity at lower cost because transmission losses are smaller. This is why large industrial consumers who take supply at high voltage (33 kV or above) pay lower tariff rates than residential consumers who receive power at 220–240 V after multiple voltage step-downs. Each step-down involves additional transformation losses and infrastructure cost. Voltage levels are therefore not merely engineering parameters — they are built into the structure of electricity tariffs and the cost of supply at each consumer category.

Modern High Voltage Direct Current (HVDC) transmission, used in several long-distance projects in India, further reduces line losses compared to AC transmission at comparable voltages, making it economically attractive for transferring bulk power across thousands of kilometres, such as from large hydro or renewable generation zones to load centres in distant states.

3.5 Conclusion

In this chapter we have discussed some concepts related to transmission of generated electricity from the generating plants to the end consumers, mainly through transmission lines using AC current.

Chapter 4: Electric Distribution System

In this chapter, we discuss aspects of electricity distribution. After the electricity gets generated and transmitted, the last task is for it to be distributed to households and offices. This is the aspect we consider here.

4.1 What is an electric distribution system

The part of an electricity power system that supplies electrical energy to individual users and consumers is called the electricity distribution system.

The distribution system includes the primary circuits and the distribution substations that supply them, the distribution transformers, the secondary circuits, including the services to the consumer and the appropriate protective and control devices.

The four general classes of individual users are residential, industrial, commercial and rural.

4.2 Alternating current or AC

Alternating current or AC is the current that reverses direction periodically, usually many times per second. This is the type of current that is commonly used for public electricity supplies, due to lower losses during transmission than DC or Direct Current. Electrical energy is ordinarily generated by public or private utility organizations and provided to different types of customers as Alternating Current. One complete period, with the current flow first in one direction and then in the opposite direction, is called a cycle. The power supply in India and many other countries is at 50 cycles per second or 50 hertz, which is different from countries like USA where 60 Hz is the common frequency.

Household power supply in India is usually at 220 to 250 volts. The voltage of an alternating current can be changed by a transformer. This simple inexpensive static device permits generation of electric power at moderate voltage, efficient transmission for many miles at high voltage and distribution and consumption at a conveniently low voltage. With direct and unidirectional current (DC current) it is not possible to use a transformer to change the voltage. On a few power lines, electrical energy is transmitted at great distances as direct current, but the electrical energy is generated as alternating current, transformed to a high voltage, then rectified to a direct current and transmitted, then transformed back to alternating current by an inverter to be transformed to a lower voltage for distribution and use.

In addition to permitting efficient transmission of energy, alternating current provides advantages to the design of generators and motors and for some purposes gives better operating characteristics.

Figure: Three-phase transformer with four wire output for 208Y/120 volt service: one wire for neutral, others for A, B and C phases. Glogger at English Wikipedia, CC BY-SA 3.0 <http://creativecommons.org/licenses/by-sa/3.0/>, via Wikimedia Commons

4.3 Three phase AC

The three-phase alternating current (AC) system is practically universal, although a few two phase and direct current (DC) systems from earlier days are still in operation. three phase transmission and sub-transmission lines require three wires termed phase conductors.

Most of the three phase distribution systems consist of three phase conductors and a common or neutral conductor, making a total of four wires. Single phase branches, consisting of two wires, supplied from three phase lines are used for single phase utilization in residences, small shops etc. Loads are connected in parallel to common supply circuits.

4.4 Distribution substation

The distribution substation is an assemblage of equipment for the purpose of switching, changing, and regulating the voltage from sub-transmission to primary distribution. More important substations are designed so that a failure of a piece of equipment in the substation or any of the sub-transmission lines to the substation will not cause an interruption of power to the load.

The primary system leaving the substation is most frequently in the 11000 to 15000 volt range A particular voltage used is 12470 volt line to line and 7200 volt line to neutral, which is conventionally written as 12470 Y/7200 volt. Some utilities use a lower voltage such as 4160 Y/2400 volts. Secondary voltages are derived from distribution transformers connected to the primary system and they usually correspond to utilization voltages.

Residential and most rural loads are supplied at 120-240 V single phase three wire systems. Commercial and small business needs are either supplied by 208Y/120 volts or 480Y/277 volts three phase four wire systems. The secondary voltage is usually used to supply multiple streetlights in addition to supplies to consumers.

4.5 Service continuity

Service continuity is the providing of uninterrupted electric power to consumers, therefore good continuity is doing this for a high percentage of the time. This is accomplished for large industrial and commercial loads by use of some form of duplicate power supply.

City commercial areas are supplied from three phase 208Y/120V grid networks. The system is arranged so that the failure of the primary feeder will not cause of loss of load on the secondary.

Commercial buildings and shopping centres are often served by spot networks. All of the transformers and protectors are at the same location.

Residential and rural loads are usually supplied by a radial system. Good continuity for them is obtained by sectionalizing the system with fuses, circuit breakers and manual switches to reduce the extent of an outage due to a failure.

4.6 Voltage Hierarchy: From Grid to Consumer

Electricity distribution is organised as a structured voltage hierarchy, with each level serving a distinct class of consumers. High voltage transmission (100 kV to 765 kV) carries bulk power over long distances with minimal losses. Medium voltage networks (typically 11 kV to 33 kV) then supply larger consumers such as industrial plants and commercial establishments directly. Finally, low voltage networks (220–240 V single phase or 415 V three phase) supply domestic and small commercial users. This hierarchy reflects both technical efficiency and cost optimisation: each voltage step-down involves transformation equipment, losses, and infrastructure investment, all of which add to the cost of electricity delivery.

This stratification has direct implications for tariff design. Large consumers taking supply at higher voltages are served with fewer transformation stages, lower losses, and simpler infrastructure. They are therefore charged lower per-unit rates than consumers served at low voltage. Tariff differentiation by voltage level is not arbitrary preference but a direct reflection of the actual cost of serving each category. The principle that "lower voltage = higher cost of supply" is one of the foundational physical reasons why electricity tariffs differ across consumer categories.

4.7 Network Design, Reliability, and Revenue

Distribution networks may be configured in several ways depending on load density, consumer type, and required reliability. In a radial system, power flows in one direction from the substation to consumers; it is simple and inexpensive, but a fault anywhere on the feeder disrupts all downstream consumers. A ring main arrangement feeds consumers from two directions so that a fault can be isolated while maintaining supply from the other side. In a mesh or interconnected network, multiple paths exist for power to reach any given consumer, providing the highest reliability at the cost of greater complexity and capital investment.

The choice of network configuration has financial consequences. Modern protection systems — including earth leakage circuit breakers, differential protection relays, and automatic sectionalising switches — allow faults to be rapidly isolated to specific sections without disrupting the entire feeder. Finer granularity of protection preserves supply continuity for a larger number of consumers during a fault, which directly reduces revenue loss for the DISCOM. Conversely, poor network design that disconnects large sections during minor faults leads to loss of billable energy and consumer dissatisfaction. Investments in reliable network design and protective systems are therefore economically justified beyond their safety benefits.

4.8 Infrastructure Design Philosophy and Cost Efficiency

Sound distribution system design balances technical performance, safety, and economic efficiency. A recurring principle in power system engineering is that unnecessarily complex network configurations — those that follow tradition rather than sound technical and economic rationale — increase both capital and operational costs without corresponding benefit. Optimal infrastructure design uses appropriate conductor sizes, correct voltage levels, and sufficient but not excessive redundancy.

The Optimal Sizing Principle

Electrical components must be sized to match the expected load — neither more nor less. Undersizing leads to overloads, insulation failure, premature equipment burnout, and costly emergency repairs, all of which increase operational expenditure and cause outages that result in lost billing revenue. Oversizing, on the other hand, wastes capital investment: a transformer rated for twice the load it will ever carry represents money tied up in unused capacity, increasing the fixed-cost component of the tariff for all consumers. In both cases the financial consequence is the same — higher electricity costs. Achieving the right size requires accurate load forecasting, phased capacity planning, and disciplined procurement — disciplines that are as much economic as they are engineering.

Material choice also has economic significance. Aluminium conductors have largely replaced older lead-sheathed cables in Indian distribution systems, since aluminium is lighter, less expensive, and easier to install. Modern polymer and XLPE insulation reduces maintenance requirements and extends cable life. These engineering choices, made at the level of individual components, aggregate into meaningful differences in the long-run cost of electricity supply and therefore in the tariffs that consumers ultimately pay.

Safety is also embedded in design standards. Voltage thresholds — such as the requirement that exposed conductive parts accessible to ordinary persons must not exceed hazardous levels — determine grounding and insulation strategies throughout the distribution network. These requirements impose specific design constraints: adequate conductor insulation, earthing systems at every substation and consumer installation, surge protection on overhead lines, and minimum clearance distances on live equipment. Each of these has a cost. However, the financial logic of meeting safety standards is compelling: the cost of compliance is predictable and manageable, while the cost of non-compliance is not. An electrical accident triggers emergency repair, liability claims, regulatory investigation, and potential prosecution. An uncontrolled fault without proper earthing can cascade into a system-wide failure destroying expensive equipment across the network. The cost of a single major safety failure typically exceeds years of compliance investment. Regulation that enforces safety standards therefore also protects the long-run financial integrity of the electricity system, and the cost of that compliance is legitimately part of the tariff that consumers pay.

4.9 Conclusion

In this chapter we have gone through aspects of an electricity distribution system to distribute electricity to domestic and industrial consumers.

Chapter 5: Electric Power Substation

In this chapter, we discuss the electric power substation, which is an important step in the transmission and distribution of electricity to consumers, as well as its main components.

Figure: An electric power substation in Chennai. Taken from Indiamart

5.1 What is an electric power substation and what is it used for

An electric power substation is an assembly of equipment in an electric power system through which electric energy is passed for transmission, distribution, interconnection, transformation, conversion and switching.

Specifically, substations are used for some or all of the following purposes:

- Connection of generators, transmission or distribution lines and loads to each other
- Transformation of power from one voltage to another
- Interconnection of alternate sources of power
- Switching for alternate connections and isolation of failed or overhead lines and equipment
- Controlling system voltage and power flows
- Reactive power compensation
- Suppression of overvoltage and detection of faults

- Monitoring and recording of information, power measurements and remote communications

Minor distribution or transmission equipment is not referred to as a substation.

5.2 Types of substations

Substations are referred to by the main duty they perform. broadly speaking, they are classified as follows:

- **Transmission substations**: which are associated with high voltage levels
- **Distribution substations**: which are associated with low voltage levels

5.3 Components of a substation

A substation includes a variety of equipment. The principal items are:

- Transformers
- Circuit breakers
- Disconnect switches

- Bus bars
- Shunt reactors
- Shunt capacitors
- Current and potential transformers
- Control and protection equipment

5.4 Substation grounding

Good substation grounding is very important for effective relaying and insulation of equipment. However, the safety of personnel is the governing criteria in the design of substation grounding. It usually consists of:

- A bare wire grid, laid in the ground
- All equipment grounding points, tanks, support structures, fences, shielding wires and poles, and so forth, securely connected to the bare wire grid.

The grounding resistance is reduced to be low enough so that a fault from high voltage to ground does not create such high potential gradients on the ground., and from the structures to ground, to create a safety hazard.

Good overhead shielding is also essential for outdoor substations, so as to virtually eliminate the possibility of lighting directly striking the equipment. Shielding is provided by overhead ground wires stretched across the substation or tall ground poles.

5.5 Conclusion

In this chapter we have discussed various concepts and components of the electric power substation, which is an important component of the electricity distribution system.

Chapter 6: Electric Energy Measurement

In this chapter, we discuss aspects related to the measurement of electrical energy consumed. This is directly linked to billing for electricity usage as well.

6.1 What is electrical energy measurement

Electrical energy measurement is the measurement of the integral with respect to time, of the power in an electrical circuit. The absolute unit of measurement of electric energy is joule, which is the charge in coulombs times the potential difference in volts. The joule, however, is too small (1 watt second) for use in commercial practice, and the more commonly used unit is the watt hour, which is $3.6 * 10^3$ joules. The most common measurement application is in the utility field.

Electric energy is one of the most accurately measured commodities sold to the general public. many methods of measurement with different degrees of accuracy are possible.

The measurements of electrical energy may be classified into two categories:

- Direct current power
- Alternating current power

The fundamental concepts of measurement are the same for both.

There are two types of methods for measuring electric energy: electric instruments and timing, and electricity meters.

6.2 Electric measurements and timing

This means making use of conventional procedures for measuring electric power and time. Typical methods are listed below:

- Measurement of energy on a direct current circuit by reading the line voltage and load current at regular intervals over a measured period of time.

- Measurement of energy on a direct current circuit by controlling the voltage and current at constant predetermined values for a predetermined time interval.

- Measurement of energy on an alternating current circuit by reading the watts input to the load at regular intervals over a measured period of time.

- Measurement of energy on an alternating current circuit by reading the watts input to the load at constant predetermined values.

- Measurement of energy by recording the watts input to the load on a linear chart progressed uniformly with time.

Figure: An electricity meter with transparent plastic case. By Zomettapuach - Own work, CC BY-SA 3.0, https://commons.wikimedia.org/w/index.php?curid=27772048

6.3 Electricity meters

Electricity meters are the most common devices for measuring the vast quantities of electric energy used by industry and the general public.

The same fundamentals of measurement apply in electric meters as for electric power measurement, but in addition, the electricity meter provides the time-integrating means necessary for electric energy measurement. A single meter is sometimes used to measure the energy consumed in two or more circuits. However, **multi-stator meters** are generally required for this purpose.

Watt hour meters are generally connected to measure the losses of their respective current circuits. The losses are extremely small compared to the total energy being measured and are present only under load conditions. Watt hour meters used for the billing of residential, commercial and industrial loads are highly developed devices.

6.4 Conclusion

In this chapter we have discussed the concepts of electricity measurement and billing of electricity usage through different types of electricity meters and other methods.

Chapter 7: Electric Protective Devices

In this chapter, we discuss various electric protective devices used in the industry.

7.1 What are electric protective devices and why are they used

These are equipment applied to electric power systems to detect abnormal and intolerable conditions and to initiate appropriate corrective action.

Disturbances in the normal operation of electric power systems may be caused:

- By natural phenomena, such as lightning, wind or snow
- By accidental means traceable to reckless drivers
- By inadvertent acts of plant maintenance personnel, or other acts of human beings

- By conditions produced in the system itself, such as switching surges, load swings or equipment failure

Protective devices must therefore be installed on a power system to ensure continuity of electric service, to limit injury to personnel and to limit damage to equipment when abnormal situations develop.

Protective devices, like any types of insurance, are applied commensurately with the degree of protection desired. For this reason, application of protective devices varies widely.

7.2 Protective zones

For the purpose of applying protection, the electric power system is divided into five major protective zones:

- Generators
- Transformers
- Buses
- Transmission and distribution lines
- Motors

Each block represents a set of protective relays and associated equipment selected to initiate correction or isolation of that area for all anticipated intolerable conditions or trouble. The detection is done by protective relays with a circuit breaker used to physically disconnect the equipment.

Figure: Electromechanical protective relays at a hydroelectric generating plant. Wtshymanski at en.wikipedia, CC BY-SA 3.0 <https://creativecommons.org/licenses/by-sa/3.0>, via Wikimedia Commons

7.3 Protective relays

These are compact analogue or digital networks connected throughout the system to detect intolerable conditions within their assigned area or zones. They operate on voltage, current, current directed power factor, power impedance, temperature and so forth, as well as combinations of these.

System faults for which the relays respond are generally short circuits between the phase conductors or between the phases and grounds. Some relays operate on imbalances between the phases, such as an open or reversed phase.

The most fundamental and widely used protection technique is the differentiator principle. The current flowing into the equipment to be protected is compared with the current flowing out. For normal and permissible operation, currents all sum to essentially zero. However, for internal trouble, they add up to flow through the relay.

While the application and protection principles are the same, the relay units may be either electromagnetic or solid-state type, also known as static.

The **plunger type** is composed of a coil, plunger and set of contacts. When current I flows in the coil, a force is produced that causes the plunger to move and close the relay contacts.

The **electromagnetic induction disk relay** responds to alternating current (AC) only. The main coil is connected to an eternal source. When current flows in the main coil, transformer action induces current in the secondary circuit connected to the upper poles.

7.4 Overcurrent protection

This must be provided on all systems to prevent abnormally high currents from overheating and causing mechanical stress on equipment. Overcurrent in a power system usually indicates that current is being diverted from its normal path by a short circuit. In low voltage, distribution type circuits, such as those found in homes, adequate overcurrent protection can be provided by fuses that melt when current exceeds a predetermined value.

Small thermal type circuit breakers also provide overcurrent protection for this class of circuit. As the size of circuits and system increases, the problems associated with the interruption of large fault currents dictate the use of power circuit breakers.

7.5 Overvoltage protection

Lightning near power lines can cause very short time overvoltages in the system and possible breakdown of the insulation.

Protection for these surges consists of lightning arresters connected between the lines and ground. Normally the insulation through these arresters prevents current flow, they momentarily pass current during the high voltage transient to limit overvoltage.

Overvoltage protection is seldom applied elsewhere except at the generators where it is part of the voltage regulation and control system.

7.6 Undervoltage protection

This must be provided on circuits supplying power to motor loads. Low voltage conditions cause motors to draw excessive currents which can damage the motors.

If a low voltage condition develops while the motor is running, the relay senses the condition and removes the motor from service.

7.7 Underfrequency protection

A loss or deficiency in the generation supply, transmission lines or other components of the system, resulting primarily from faults, can leave the system with an excess of load.

Solid state digital type under frequency relays are connected at various points in the system to detect the resulting decline in the normal system frequency. They operate to disconnect loads or to separate the system with areas so that the available generation equals the load until a balance is established.

7.8 Reverse current protection

This is provided when a change in the normal direction of current indicates an abnormal condition in the system. In an AC circuit, reverse current implies a phase shift of the current of nearly 180 degrees from normal. This is actually a change in direction of power flow and can be detected by AC directional relays.

7.9 Protective Systems and Their Economic Role

Protective devices such as fuses, circuit breakers, overcurrent relays, and earth leakage protection are typically discussed in terms of their safety function:

they detect abnormal conditions and disconnect the affected part of the system before damage or danger occurs. But these devices also serve a critical economic function that is less commonly appreciated. By isolating faults rapidly and precisely, protection systems limit the financial consequences of system disturbances in three distinct ways.

First, they prevent equipment damage. An uncleared fault — a short circuit or overload that is not quickly interrupted — can burn out transformers, destroy cables, and damage switchgear. Repair or replacement of major equipment is expensive and time-consuming. A well-coordinated protection scheme that trips a fuse or breaker within milliseconds of a fault can limit damage to a small, replaceable component rather than allowing it to cascade into catastrophic and costly equipment failure.

Second, they limit outage scope and duration. A highly selective protection scheme disconnects only the faulted section, preserving supply to all other consumers on the network. A poorly designed scheme with coarse protection may disconnect an entire feeder or substation when only one small branch has faulted. Every consumer disconnected during that outage represents lost billing revenue for the DISCOM —

energy that has been purchased from generators but cannot be sold. Over a year, repeated incidents of unnecessarily wide outages due to inadequate protection represent a measurable revenue gap.

Third, protection systems reduce regulatory and liability exposure. India's Electricity (Rights of Consumers) Rules 2020 set standards for supply quality and interruptions; utilities that exceed permissible outage limits face penalties. Adequate protection infrastructure is therefore not an optional investment but a regulatory requirement, the cost of which forms part of the legitimate capital base on which tariffs are calculated.

This creates a clear engineering-economic logic: investing in well-designed, coordinated protection systems reduces long-run costs — in equipment repair, lost revenue, and regulatory penalties — that would otherwise exceed the investment itself. Protection systems are, in this sense, revenue protection systems as much as they are safety systems. A DISCOM that treats protective device maintenance and system protection coordination as a cost to be minimised is ultimately increasing its own financial risk.

7.10 Electrical Accidents and Safety Voltages

Electricity does not cause many accidents, and relatively fewer fatal accidents, but it is nevertheless a serious source of potential danger. Electrical hazards, unlike many mechanical hazards, are not usually obvious: a live conductor does not differ in appearance from a dead conductor, and the absence of earthing on a metal enclosure may pass unnoticed until it is too late. When such metalwork is touched and found to be dangerously live, electric shock can cause death within a few minutes.

Statistics show that although the number of electrical accidents is typically a small proportion of total accidents in any field of activity, the percentage of electrical accidents that prove fatal is often much higher than the fatality rate for accidents taken as a whole. Most accidents, in a worldwide context, occur on alternating current electrical systems between 125 V and 660 V — the voltage range most commonly used in industrial, commercial, and domestic settings. It is important to note that low voltage is quite sufficiently dangerous to cause fatal shock, despite the fact that at times shocks may be received at such voltages that cause only minor discomfort.

The fundamental approach to electrical safety is the adoption, wherever possible, of supply voltages below the level at which lethal current can pass through the human body. The "safety extra-low voltage" recommended by the International Electrotechnical Commission is 50 V. In practice, portable lamps and tools are commonly supplied at extra-low voltage derived from a double-wound transformer with the centre point of the secondary winding connected to earth, so that the maximum shock voltage to earth does not exceed 55 V. For much fixed electrical equipment and some portable apparatus, the use of a non-lethal supply voltage is not practicable for technical or economic reasons, and special attention must therefore be given to other safety measures.

7.11 Occupational Categories and Safety in Low-Voltage Distribution

Persons exposed to the risk of electrical accident can be divided into two main categories. The first consists of those trained and experienced in electrical work, employed in it as their trade or profession. The second consists of persons unskilled in electricity who use plant, machinery, and apparatus energised by electricity, and who are at risk from faults in that equipment or from its misuse.

In low-voltage distribution systems for domestic and industrial purposes, it is not uncommon for no special provision beyond the transformer to be made for overload protection, relying instead on fuses as the tripping mechanism. The slow operation of screw-in or clip-type fuses can result in arcing or flashover followed by burning of the contacts, which is dangerous for service personnel. This danger becomes more acute as the system becomes more heavily loaded.

The following safety precautions should be observed in low-voltage distribution work: (a) All work must be carried out by experienced electricians fully familiar with the technical aspects and possible dangers; the risk of accidental contact with live components must be emphasised in all instructions. (b) Handles or switches for operating the equipment must be so constructed that cut-outs or fuses cannot be inserted or removed using makeshift tools, and handles should be provided with hand and lower arm protection of leather or other heat-resisting material, affording protection at least to the elbow. (c) As far as possible, all installations must be laid out so that contact with live parts during normal operation is prevented. The fitting of flashproof boxes which, when opened, cause the current to be cut off, eliminates much of this danger; suitable apertures permit the introduction of test leads to verify whether contacts are live.

In the event of an overload or short circuit, protective equipment must be dimensioned so that it can safely interrupt breaking currents which may range from 1,250 A to 10,000 A or more, depending on fault conditions. If the breaking capacity is not adequate, arcing may occur and cause fire or explosion, damaging equipment and injuring workers. In large installations, protection should be graded so that each overload protection device has a rated current one or two steps higher than its downstream neighbour. This ensures selective protection: only the device immediately upstream of the fault trips, localising the effects of the fault and allowing other circuits to continue operating. It should also be ensured that under normal operating conditions the voltage drop between the distribution panel and consumer appliances does not exceed 1.5% of the rated voltage; where the consumer appliances are motors, a voltage drop of up to 3% can normally be accepted.

7.12 Investigation of Electrical Accidents

Most countries now have legislation administered by a government inspectorate or independent body to ensure that electricity is installed and used safely. In India, the Central Electricity Authority (CEA) sets technical standards for electrical installations, and state electrical inspectorates investigate accidents and enforce compliance. When starting an accident investigation, the inspector must address several aspects: (a) whether statutory regulations appear to have been breached, and if so by whom — a decision must be made whether to take legal action, influenced by the severity of the breach, whether it appears deliberate or due to carelessness, and the previous compliance record; (b) whether any defect in apparatus warrants a prohibition on further use or requires improvements; (c) where no statutory contravention has occurred, whether to make recommendations designed to improve safety; (d) the level of knowledge, training, and experience possessed by the injured persons and by those supervising the work, which is of particular importance where electrical work is being carried out and where young persons are involved; and (e) where basic design or construction defects are found in apparatus made in large quantities, whether the manufacturers should be asked to advise their agents and distributors of the risk so that further sales can be interrupted and existing users warned.

7.13 Conclusion

In this chapter we have discussed different types of electricity protective devices such as protective relays and principles of how they work. The following sections address the important related topic of electrical accidents, safety in low-voltage distribution systems, and the investigation of electrical accidents.

Chapter 8: History of Electricity Supply Legislation in India

In this chapter, we discuss the history of the electricity supply legislation in India from the British times.

8.1 History of electricity supply legislation in India

The British rulers introduced electricity to India, starting from a demonstration of electric lighting in Calcutta in 1879 and a company getting the license to supply electricity in Calcutta in 1897 followed soon by Bombay.

The **Indian Electricity Act 1910** was one of the early laws related to the regulation of electricity supply in India. It had the provision for issuing licenses to private companies for supply to particular areas, mostly urban areas.

After India became independent, the constitution of India placed electricity supply under the concurrent list, as a responsibility shared between the central and state governments.

The **Electricity Supply Act 1948** was introduced soon after independence. Under this act, the Central Electricity Authority or CEA at the national level and state electricity boards were set up at the state level, their job being to expand the supply of electricity to different areas within each state. These boards were all nationalized and electricity supply was a state monopoly, with licenses provided to other players by the state. Soon, the smaller towns and villages also gradually came to be electrified.

However, there were problems with the electricity boards such as that of efficiency. There was extended loss of electricity supply or what was known as load shedding or power cuts in many areas, particularly bringing misery to the people during the hot Indian summers.

In 1991, the **liberalization and reform** of the the Indian economy took place. As part of this, many of the state electricity boards, many of which had inefficiencies and were in a not so good financial position, were restructured or privatized fully or partly as corporations.

Private players or independent power producers were also allowed in electricity power plants such as thermal, hydro, wind and solar energy generation plants.

The **Electricity Regulatory Act 1998** was set up that created the **central electricity regulatory commission (CERC)** and **state electricity regulatory commissions (SERC)** for regulating the electricity supply. These had the role of setting the electricity tariff for consumers such as households, industry and agricultural sector and also adjudicating all kinds of disputes related to electricity supply. Reforms acts were brought in different states as well, such as the **Delhi Electricity Reforms Act 2000** and **Uttar Pradesh Electricity Reforms Act 1999**.

This was followed by the **Electricity Act 2003**, which liberalized the electricity regime especially in the areas of electricity generation and distribution.

8.2 Background to the Electricity Act 2003

To further make the electricity supply efficient and to help with some shortcomings in earlier legislation, the Electricity Act 2003 was introduced by the government and approved in the Indian parliament. This encouraged the entry of more private players in the electricity supply and generation. The generators of electricity were free to sell the generated electricity to any customer at any location or region. This was termed as **open access** of the transmission and distribution of electricity.

The need for a license for most cases of generation of electricity was dispensed with. However, the distribution and transmission and trading of electricity still do need a license.

Later, the concept of **customer satisfaction**, consumer protection and grievance redressal in the area of electricity supply was also given prominence, and customer grievance mechanisms were instituted.

DISCOMs or Electricity Distribution Companies were set up to interact with the end customers and the power generation units. State Electricity Regulatory Commissions or SERCs were also set up whose task was to prevent abuse of monopoly power by the electricity companies.

8.6 Conclusion

In this chapter we have gone through the history of electricity related regulation in India, leading up to the Electricity Act 2003. In the following chapter we will study the act in more detail.

Chapter 9: Electricity Act 2003

In this chapter, we discuss the Electricity Act 2003, which is the main law covering generation, transmission and distribution of electricity.

9.1 Introduction to the Electricity Act 2003

The Electricity Act 2003 consolidates the law related to regulate the generation, transmission and distribution of electricity in India. It also has sections related to electricity tariff and revenue policies.

It is the consolidated version of some earlier existing electricity acts in India such as the Indian Electricity Act 1910, The Electricity (Supply) Act 1948 and the Electricity Regulatory Commission Act 1998.

The Electricity Act, 2003

MINISTRY OF LAW AND JUSTICE
(Legislative Department)

New Delhi, the 2nd June, 2003.Jyaistha 12, 1925 (Saka)

The following Act of Parliament received the assent of the President on the 26th May, 2003, and is hereby published for general information:

THE ELECTRICITY ACT, 2003
[No.36 of 2003]

[26th May, 2003]

An Act to consolidate the laws relating to generation, transmission, distribution, trading and use of electricity and generally for taking measures conducive to development of electricity industry, promoting competition therein, protecting interest of consumers and supply of electricity to all areas, rationalization of electricity tariff, ensuring transparent policies regarding subsidies, promotion of efficient and environmentally benign policies, constitution of Central Electricity Authority, Regulatory Commissions and establishment of Appellate Tribunal and for matters connected therewith or incidental thereto.

Be it enacted by Parliament in the Fifty-fourth Year of the Republic of India as follows:-

PART I

PRELIMINARY

Section 1. (Short title, extent and commencement) --- (1) This Act may be called the Electricity Act, 2003.

(2) It extends to the whole of India except the State of Jammu and Kashmir.

(3) It shall come into force on such date as the Central Government may, by notification, appoint:

Provided that different dates may be appointed for different provisions of this Act and any reference in any such provision to the commencement of this Act shall be construed as a reference to the coming into force of that provision.

Figure: Front Page of the Electricity Act 2003

9.2 Features of the Electricity Act 2003

Some features of the Electricity Act 2003 are as follows:

- **No license is needed for generation of electricity**. Any generating company may establish, operate and maintain a generating power station without a licence. However, it should comply with the technical standards relating to connectivity with the grid. Hydro-projects, however, need clearance from the Central Electricity Authority (CEA). Generation from renewable sources to be promoted. However, nuclear power stations can only be operated by government companies.

- **License is mandatory for the transmission and distribution and trading** in electricity. Exceptions are informed by authorised commissions through notifications.

- There shall be a **Central transmission utility** (CTU) in the centre and **State transmission utilities** (STUs) in the states. Transmission utility at the central and state level to be a government company with responsibility of planned and coordinated development of transmission network.

- **Load dispatch** to be regulated along with transmission, also by a government company. Open access is provided to transmission lines for distribution licensees and generation companies.

- Setting up of **State Electricity Regulatory Commission** (SERC) within 6 months in each state. Joint commissions can be set up if states agree.

- **Distribution of electricity** to be regulated by SERCs, along with the tariffs. Distribution licenses can be suspended upon holding an enquiry. **Metering** of electricity supplied is made mandatory.

- Central Government may make region-wise demarcation of the country and modifications for efficient, economical and **integrated transmission and supply of electricity**, and also to facilitate voluntary inter-connections and co-ordination of facilities for the inter-State, regional and inter-regional generation and transmission of electricity.

- **Open access** in transmission with provision for surcharge for taking care of current level of cross-subsidy, with the surcharge being gradually phased out.

- The state governments are required to unbundle **State Electricity Boards (SEBs)**. However, they may continue with them as distribution licensees and state transmission utilities. Provision for scheme to privatize the SEBs.

- **Appellate tribunal** set up to hear appeals against the orders of CERC and SERC's.

- Penalties for **thefts of electricity** made more stringent. Provision for compounding of offenses related to electricity theft. Pilferage of electricity can be punished with imprisonment. Special courts can be convened for electricity offenses.

- **Trading of electricity** is recognised with the **regulatory commission** authorised to fix ceiling on trading margins to prevent price volatility. Licenses to be given for trading. Regulatory commission to promote a market for trading.

- For **rural and remote areas**, stand-alone system for generation and distribution is permitted. Thrust by central and state governments to complete **rural electrification** and provide for management of rural distribution by panchayat, cooperative societies, NGOs, franchisees etc. No license needed for generation and distribution of electricity in rural areas.

- Central government to prepare **National Electricity Policy** and **Tariff Policy** in consultation with state governments. They will also prepare a national policy for rural areas, with focus on non-conventional energy sources.

- Regulatory commission to determine tariffs and **tariff principles**. Cross-subsidies to reduce and tariff moved closer to actual cost of supply.

- **Central Electricity Authority** (CEA) to be the technical advisor of central and state governments, CERC and SERCs, and to prepare the National Electricity Plan. CEA to specify standards for construction of electrical plants and transmission lines, safety standards and meters.

- Provisions have been made for **consumer protection**, with specified time frame to give new electricity connection. **Grievance redressal forum** to be set up for consumer grievances.

Licensees must meet the standards set up by the regulatory commission.

Figure: First page of the Electricity Consumer Rules 2020

9.3 The Electricity (Rights of Consumers) Rules 2020

The Electricity Rules 2020 were brought by the Indian government to foster better accountability to consumers of electricity in India by the distribution companies, and also include a grievance mechanism for consumer grievances. It covers areas such as connection, metering, billing and payment and the standards of performance to which the licensees (distribution companies) shall be held accountable. These rules are expected to further benefit the consumers and lead to increased accountability and transparency in electricity supply.

9.4 Conclusion

In this chapter we have discussed the Electricity Act 2003 and the Electricity Rules 2020. We have also briefly discussed some features of the act.

Chapter 10: National Tariff Policy

In this chapter we discuss some features of the national tariff policy, which regulates the electricity tariffs in India at different levels.

10.1 Objective of the national tariff policy

The objectives include ensuring continuous availability of electricity at reasonable prices, ensure financial viability of the electricity sector by attracting investments, promote transparency in regulation of electricity, and promote quality improvements and efficiency.

10.2 Summary of the tariff policy

The national electricity tariff policy lays down certain principles for the fixing of tariffs at various levels. These include the following:

- Ensuring a good ROI or return of investment

- Ensuring an equity:debt ratio of 70:30 for financing capital cost of projects
- Notifying the rates of depreciation of assets
- Structuring the debt in such a way that tariffs are reduced.
- Managing foreign exchange risks as applicable.
- Evolving performance norms for operations so as to promote efficiency.
- Renovation and modernization of the power sector and its components.
- Tariff structuring and pricing principles for generation, transmission and distribution and various issues related to each of them.
- Linking the tariffs to the cost of providing the service.
- Principles for fixing surcharge for different classes of users: households, industries and agricultural users.
- Fixing the trading margins and monitoring the trading of electricity.

The cost of supply of electricity to end consumers may be calculated by the following surcharge formula:

$$S = T - [\, C\,(1 + L/100) + D\,]$$

where:

- S is the surcharge
- T is the tariff payable by the relevant category of consumers
- C is the Weighted average cost of power purchase of top 5% at the margin excluding liquid fuel-based generation and renewable power
- D is the wheeling charge
- L is the system losses for the applicable voltage level, expressed as a percentage

10.3 Conclusion

In this chapter we have discussed some salient features and principles of the tariff policy, that seeks to regulate the tariffs of electricity at various levels and improve the efficiency, with a view to keeping tariffs reasonable for different kinds of consumers.

Chapter 11: Regulatory Framework

In this chapter we discuss the overall regulatory framework for electricity in India. This specifies who makes and who regulates policies related to electricity and tariff in India.

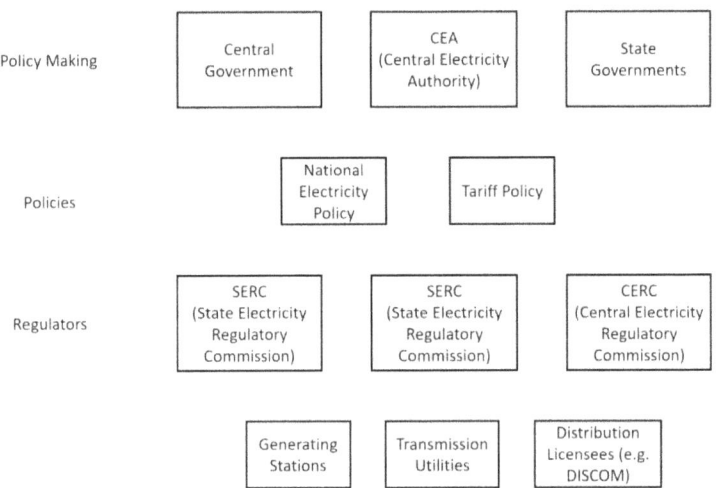

Figure: Structure of the current regulatory framework for electricity in India

11.1 Components of the Regulatory Framework

The components of the regulatory framework for electricity in India include the following:

- **Central Government and State Governments**: Since electricity is in the concurrent list, it is the responsibility of both central as well as state governments. In both cases the ministries related to power in centre and state governments handle electricity matters.

- **Central Electricity Authority (CEA)**: This was established by the Electricity Supply Act 1948 and its role is to advise the government about technical matters related to generation, transmission and distribution of electricity, standards for construction of power grids and electricity lines and policies related to tariff. It has a role in managing the integration of the national electricity grid and the state grids.

- **Central electricity regulatory commission (CERC)**: This was set up by the Electricity Act 2003. Its main role is the regulation of electricity tariffs for central-owned generating stations as well at inter-state levels, along with transmission and trading at the inter-state levels. It also regulates the amount of subsidy at the national level. Additionally, it has the role of adjudicating disputes related to electricity supply and tariff.

- **State electricity regulatory commissions (SERC)**: These were also set up by the Electricity Act 2003 and regulate matters related to tariffs and subsidies at the state level. Particularly, it regulates the amount to be charged from the consumers.

11.2 Conclusion

In this chapter, we have briefly gone through the different elements of the regulatory framework for electricity in India.

Chapter 12: Regulation of Electricity Transmission, Distribution and Trading

In this chapter we discuss about the regulatory framework for transmission, distribution and trading of electricity in India.

12.1 Overview of transmission regulation as per the electricity act

Transmission of electricity is a licensed activity and the licensee company has to adhere to the tariff policy, national electricity policy and the relevant CERC and SERC regulations. CERC provides the licenses at the inter-state level and SERCs provides the licenses for transmission lines within the state.

As per the electricity act 2003, a Central transmission utility (CTU) in the centre and State transmission utilities (STUs) in the states is constituted.

Power Grid Corporation of India is the public sector company owning and managing the inter-state transmission. It has the responsibility of planned and coordinated development of transmission network. Its responsibilities include providing a transmission system as well as the establishment and maintenance of regional and national power grid to facilitate transfer of power across states and regions as needed.

Within the different states, the transmission systems are owned and managed by state transmission utilities which are licensed.

As per the electricity act, load dispatch to be regulated along with transmission, also by a government company.

Open access is provided to transmission lines by the transmission licensee to the distribution licensees and generation companies.

The transmission licensee must also provide for consumer protection and grievance redressal.

12.2 Overview of distribution regulation as per the electricity act

Distribution of electricity is a licensed activity. The licensee company has to get the license from the CERC or SERC and comply with the regulations and policies. Sale and distribution of electricity to the final consumers (such as industrial, agricultural and residential homes) are both covered under the same license. Distribution and supply of electricity are segregated, and multiple suppliers or distributors of electricity (such as DISCOMs) can use the distribution network but have to get separate licenses.

12.3 Overview of trading regulation as per the electricity act

Trading means the purchase of electricity either from generating stations or from distribution licensees for sale to the end customers who may be residential homes or agricultural or industrial customers. Trading of electricity is also a licensed activity. The licensee has to get the license for trading from the CERC or SERCs and comply with all the relevant regulations.

12.4 Conclusion

We have discussed about the regulatory framework for transmission, distribution and trading of electricity in India as per the electricity act 2003.

Chapter 13: Some Considerations for Setting Electricity Tariffs

Electricity tariffs in India reflect a complex interplay of technical parameters, regulatory goals, political priorities, and social equity. While consumers see the final bill amount, the underlying pricing mechanisms involve technical, economic, and legal considerations. This chapter aims to provide a unified view combining traditional engineering factors like load factor and diversity with contemporary consumer-facing tariff structures across Indian states.

13.1 Introduction to Electricity Tariffs and Load Factor: Why a Flat Rate is Insufficient

Electricity cannot be stored on a large scale economically, unlike water or fuel. Generation must match real-time demand. Therefore having a flat rate or fixed rate per unit for tariff does not serve the purpose. Hence, a two-part tariff or dynamic tariff can be better suited.

Hence, tariffs must recover both:

- Fixed costs (e.g. infrastructure, staff, transformers)
- Variable costs (e.g. fuel, maintenance)

This leads to the adoption of **two-part tariffs**.

13.2 The Two-Part Tariff System

The concept of two-part tariff is based on two costs: the first part is covered by an annual amount, and the second part is charged per unit used.

This system has:

- **Fixed Charge**: Reflects the cost of infrastructure, levied per month based on sanctioned load.
- **Energy Charge**: Variable part, billed based on actual usage (in kWh).

Many states combine this with **slab-wise (telescopic)** energy charges, where unit cost increases with higher consumption:

Example:

- ₹3/unit for 0–100 units
- ₹5/unit for 101–200 units
- ₹7/unit for 201–400 units

Two part tariffs are usually of different types: industrial and domestic and agricultural farms.

- An industrial two-part tariff is always based on the maximum demand, either in KVA or KW. It is more usual nowadays to base the fixed charge on KVA so that the supply authority is compensated for any consumer taking his supply at a low power factor. Another method is to allow for power factor by means of an additional clause, varying it per unit by an amount of a power factor above or below a datum, say 0.8. In this way, the consumer is recompensated if he has a high value of the power factor.

- The maximum demand figure is obtained by means of a maximum demand indicator for a given time period (such as 15-30 minutes), which gives the highest load, weather in KW or KVA as per the tariff.

- Special tariffs are in many cases offered to consumers with favourable loads. Bulk supply tariffs to large consumers also include a clause varying the consumption figure per unit according to the price of electricity generation such as coal above or below a certain price per ton. Industrial two-part tariffs are based to a large extent on the actual cost of the service. For smaller consumers, fixed simple flat rate charges may be used.

13.3 Technical Concepts Affecting Tariffs

Load factor: This measures how efficiently a consumer uses maximum demand capacity.

This can be defined as the average load compared with the maximum load for any given period. It is calculated as follows:

Load factor = (Actual energy consumed) / (Maximum demand * Time in hours of the period)

or

Load Factor = (Total Energy Used in Period) / (Maximum Load × Hours)

Higher load factors reduce average cost per unit for the utility.

The load factor for a consumer may vary widely from 5% to 80%, but generally it is 10% for lighting only to 40% for industrial or heating loads. Some industries have a 24-hour load, and in that case the load factor will be very high.

Because of this two-part nature of the cost of supplying electrical energy, the actual load factor has a direct effect on the cost per unit, since the fixed or standing charge to cover the first cost is divided into all the units used during that period. The more units used and higher the load factor, the lower will be the fixed cost per unit. Hence, it is the aim of every supply engineer to make the load factor as high as possible, and they can offer special inducements to those consumers who enable this.

Power Factor: Relevant for industrial users. Poor power factor leads to inefficient energy usage.

Diversity Factor: This is the ratio of the sum of individual peak demands to the actual system peak. This helps reduce total system capacity requirement.

The diversity of a supply load is given by the diversity factor, which is calculated as follows:

Diversity factor = (Sum of consumers maximum demands) / (Maximum demand on system)

The average consumers load factor must be calculated with reference to actual consumption and not merely as a numerical average.

Utilities may offer **rebates for good load factor/power factor** and penalize poor ones.

13.4 Factors Influencing Tariff Design

These include the following:

- Operational efficiency of DISCOMs
- Plant Load Factor of power generators
- T&D Losses (technical + theft losses)
- Auxiliary power consumption
- Coal and fuel prices
- Interest and depreciation on capital assets

13.5 Rate Schedules for State Electricity Boards: The UPSEB Example

Since the creation of the state electricity boards in the 1950s, tariff revisions have been done from time to time on an ad hoc basis, so as to balance the revenue and expenditure. These did not take into account the actual cost and operating structure. Some boards in the 1980s appointed Tariff Rationalization Committees (TRCs) of experienced engineers and experts to make recommendations to rationalize tariffs on a long-term basis.

Various norms were set for the efficient working of thermal power stations and transmission and distribution systems. This provided a safeguard to consumers to not be overcharged by the state electricity boards.

For example, the 1985 TRC of Uttar Pradesh State Electricity Board (UPSEB) set the following norms:

Parameters	Actual figures (1980s)	Norm from TRC
PLF of thermal plants	40.5% Units of 200/210 MW 61.07%	For units <200MW 57.07%,
Auxiliary Thermal power station	13.3%	10%
Auxiliary Hydel power station	1.5%	1%
T&D Losses	19%	17%
Coal Consumption Per Unit	0.833 Kg	0.74 kg
O&M expenses	5p/unit	3.75p/unit
Established cost	11p/unit	7.77p/unit

From the above figures it can be seen that the TRC has not passed any burden to consumers for a fall in efficiency in operating conditions existing in UPSEB. The weighed average cost of energy/unit, based on the above norms assumed by TRC, comes to 78.65 p/unit including 3% net surplus as required under the Electricity (Supply) Act 1948. Based on this figure, the entire rate structure has been built.

The Electricity Supply (Consumers) Regulations, 1984 says the following:

In exercise of the powers under sections 49 and 79 of the Electricity (Supply) Act 1948, the Uttar Pradesh State Electricity Board makes the following regulations with a view to lay down the terms and conditions for supply of electricity to persons other than licensees:

- *These regulations may be called the Electricity (Consumers) Regulations 1984.*

- *Unless otherwise provided in any individual contract, all the provisions of the regulations shall apply to all kinds of electrical supply to all classes of consumers as if they were part of the contract between the electricity board and the consumer.*

- *The conditions of supply enforced by the board from 1966 are replaced by these regulations.*

- *Important matters like malpractice, theft of electricity, requisite of supply, estimate of the cost of supply line chargeable to the consumer, etc are provided in the definitions.*

- *Guidelines for the assessment under annexure 1, assessment and appeal, discontinuance of supply in case of malpractice and pilferage of electricity, meters, payment of bills, tariff, agreement, consumption of security deposit, testing of installations prior to connection, application for alteration and shifting of service line or meter, private tube well or pumping sets, small and medium industrial power consumers up to 75 KW/100BHP, steel arc furnace industries, large or heavy power consumers above 75 KW, application of additional load or reduction in load, reconnection of supply, requisition of supply have been provided for by the UPSEB under conditions of supply effective from July 1984.*

- *Industrial consumers more than 75 KW and up to 200 KW and more than 200 KW have been provided special provision in the rate of charge as well in minimum consumption guarantee, billable demand. Incentive to new industry in the form of 10% rebate has been provided.*

- *Separate tariff under rate schedule HV 3A and HV 3B has been provided for railway traction*

- *In the rate schedule of private tube well or pumping sets for irrigation purposes, while energy will be supplied at a single point, the rate of charge has been reduced at Rs 180/BHP/year chargeable at the rate of Rs 15 per BHP/month.*

- *In the commercial list and power while energy will be supplied to consumers at a single point, the minimum charge of Rs 25/KW/month for cinemas and theatres and for others Rs 60 per connection per month have been provided.*

- *The rate of fuel surcharge worked out by the state electricity board shall be fixed and binding on the consumer. This is applicable on all consumers governed by rate schedule HV 1/ HV2/ HV 3A and 3B. The fuel surcharge will continue to be charged at the same rate unless an increase is declared.*

13.6 Considerations for formulation of a rational electricity tariff

The considerations for formulation of electricity tariff are contained in section 23 of Indian Electricity Act 2010 (IEA 1910) and Sections 49 and 59 of Electricity (Supply) Act 1948.

The salient features of the provisions are as follows:

- The tariff will be such that the coordinated development of the supply and distribution of electricity within the state is the most efficient and economical manner, with particular reference to areas not adequately served currently.

- It leaves a surplus of not less than 3% or such higher percentage as fixed by the state government of the value of the fixed assets of the board in service at the beginning of each year.

- The board shall not show any undue preference to any person.

- The extension of supply of electricity to sparsely developed areas shall be done.

Besides the above statutory conditions, other relevant factors are that the operation of the system must be based on reasonably efficient operating conditions, i.e. any inefficiencies caused due to the laxity on part of the state electricity boards shall not be passed on to the consumers. Further, the state may be facing acute shortage of power. Resources of the state being limited, it is necessary to attract aid from external sources and the tariff structure will have to take into consideration the terms and conditions of such aid giving agencies. Further, due to continuing shortage of energy, all out efforts should be made towards cutting down wasteful use of energy by means of incentives and penalties.

13.7 Factors for a reasonably efficient operation

In order to identify the factors that make a reasonably efficient operation for production of energy, the various components of the cost of energy need to be studied.

It is seen from the historical data that out of the various factors, interest and depreciation constitute about 35% to 39% of the total cost. These items are, however, dependent on the rate of interest and depreciation that are fixed by the state governments or central government or other loaning agencies. Therefore, these rates are not in control of the electricity board.

However, if the quantum of energy generated with the same installed capacity is more, the cost percent will go down as both these charges are fixed. Similarly, impact of 3% surplus will also be influenced by the quantum of energy generated. Purchase of power from outside sources, however, depends upon the shortage of power in the state. Also, lower auxiliary consumption and transmission and distribution losses mean that there is more availability of power for distribution for the same installed capacity. Therefore, in deciding the reasonably efficient operation, the following factors are relevant:

- Plant load factor
- Consumption of electricity in auxiliaries in paise per unit of energy generated
- Transmission and distribution losses of the system
- Oil consumption per unit of energy generated
- Coal consumption per unit of energy generated

- Operation and maintenance cost
- Establishment cost

13.8 Alternative methods of costing

In order to work out the average cost of energy for purposes of fixing the sale rate, the following approaches are possible:

- The cost can be based on the **historical cost or investment** made till date. While this will give the correct costing as far as immediate cost is concerned, it will not be able to account for increased cost of inputs and plants of higher per KW cost coming into operation. Hence, this rate cannot remain stable, particularly when addition to system capacity are substantial each year as in some electricity boards.

- The cost of energy can be based on the **future capital costs** likely to be incurred. This correctly represents the cost of power in future if the plant is set up now. This is also referred to as **Long Range Marginal Cost**. Based on economic theories, application of long-range marginal cost is considered to be reasonable for maximum exploitation of available economic resources, as it correctly gives cost signal to the consumer. However, the cost per unit on this basis typically becomes very high. This is because of higher capital costs per KW of capacity being added.

- The cost can be calculated on the basis of **capital cost already incurred and also the capital cost to be incurred** in the near future. This method will give a cost which will be stable for some time, assuming the estimated project costs remain stable as well. The committee considered that it is in the interests of the state that the tariff is fixed such that it will be stable say for the next 4-5 years. The committee noted that the cost of energy based on past investment suffers because new additions are higher in terms of per kw cost. Hence the committee considered it desirable to calculate the cost of energy on the basis of capital already invested and proposed to be invested during a five year plan period.

13.9 Estimate of Future Cost

The future cost of energy is calculated as per the five-year plan projection by the state electricity boards as well as outlined by the committee.

13.10 Categorization of Consumers

The tariff schedule in force before 1986 had 18 defined categories of consumers. In addition, a special category has been created temporarily so long as power restrictions on them made it necessary. The committee tried to regroup the consumers with the following basic considerations:

- Consumers having similar load characteristics are brought into the same category as far as practicable.
- A consumer is covered only in one category if he does not have use of energy for dissimilar purposes on a large scale.
- Ambiguities if any present in the categorization are removed.

On this basis consumers were regrouped into 12 categories, with the following factors:

- **Domestic light, fan and power consumers**: Presently all shops, restaurants and other such commercial establishments in a town having population less than 1 lakh and load below 2 KW are included in this category.

- **Commercial light, fan and power consumers and mixed load consumers**. These include consumers of lights, fan and power loads other than industrial and domestic. This also includes all offices except that of the electricity boards. Power for construction projects of private or public projects or other work of commercial institutions are also included. All non-domestic consumers can be divided into two sub-categories: energy for works of public welfare including schools and colleges, universities and their hostels, hospitals etc run by state or central governments or recognized charitable institutions, public libraries, museums, non-commercial institutes and societies.

- **Small and medium power consumers**. All light and fan consumption by them for running the industry is billed using the same tariff as for power.

- **Public lamps**: This category includes public lamps

- **PTW and pump sets** upto 15 HP, tubewells, pump canals and irrigation schemes of state and central governments upto 100 BHP.

- **Large and heavy power consumers**. These are in two categories: Large power consumers who have contracted load about 100 BHP (75 KW) upto 200 KW (235 KVA) and the other for those having contracted demand about 200 KW (235 KVA). These are subject to power cuts and peak load restrictions. They can be further subdivided into subcategories based on use patterns. World bank tubewells constructed by irrigation department are also considered as heavy power consumers.

- **Railway traction loads**

- **Janata connections**

- **Arc or industrial furnace, rolling and re-rolling mills and mini steel plants above 75 KW/100 HP.**

13.11 Restriction on Release of Connections

In order to ensure better supply conditions, lower system losses and ensure better system stability, the following restrictions are proposed on the release of connections:

- Domestic and non-domestic connections above 2KW/3KWA should be released on three phase

- All connections above 100 KVA and upto 1000 KVA should not be released at voltage lower than 11 KV

- All connections above 1000 KVA and upto 10 MVA should not be released at voltage lower than 33 KV

- All loads above 10 MVA should not be released at a voltage lower than 132 KV

- In views of the obsolete nature of DC converting equipment and very high maintenance costs involved, all existing DC consumers should be asked to change over to AC system which will be both in interest of the supplier as well as the consumer. There is a ban already on release of new DC connections.

13.12 Proposed Rates of Security Deposit

The main considerations for proposed rates of security deposit are as follows:

- In case of large and heavy power consumers, the security deposit should be roughly equal to one month's bill.

- In case of consumers of streetlights, PTWs and small and medium power consumers being billed on a monthly basis, the security deposit should be roughly equivalent to 1.5 months' bill.

- In case of non-domestic consumers proposed to be billed on a monthly basis, the security deposit should be roughly equivalent to two months' bill.

- In case of domestic and non-domestic consumers being billed on a bi-monthly basis, the security deposit should be roughly equivalent to four months' bill.

- Presently no security is levied on central and state government departments.

Presently the state electricity board allows interest of 3% per annum on the amount of security deposit above Rs 100. The commission felt that the consumers who are entitled to this interest must get it timely and regularly. It will be credited to the electricity bills.

13.13 Fuel Surcharge

The fuel surcharge due to increased cost of coal, furnace oil and freight is amalgamated into the tariff in UP State Electricity Board up to 1980. For further increases, the fuel surcharge is worked out as per the formulae given below:

- For every 10% increase in the delivered cost of coal grade 'C' and freight charge of delivering coal up to Parki power station, the fuel surcharge shall be levied at Rs 1.34 per unit.

- In addition to the above, for every 10% increase in the delivered cost of furnace oil from Koyali, Gujarat and freight charges up to Parki Power Station, fuel surcharge shall be levied at 0.44 p per unit.

- Escalation in the cost of coal, oil and freight less than 5% will be ignored, and 5% or more must be deemed as 10%.

- Chief controller of Audits and Accounts or chief accounts officer of the state electricity board shall work out the rate of fuel surcharge and intimate the increase to the field officers.

- The increase in fuel surcharge shall be applicable to all consumers governed by rate schedule HV-1, HV-2, HV-3A and 3B.

- The delivered cost of coal and oil at the power station include cost ex colliery or ex refinery.

- Amount of fuel surcharge shall not be accounted for towards minimum charge or minimum consumption guarantee.

- No relaxation or rebate to the development rebate for taking supplies at higher voltage etc shall be admissible on the amount of fuel surcharge

- Fuel surcharge shall also be subjected to the levy of additional charge for delayed payment of bills

- The rate of fuel surcharge worked out by the state electricity board shall be final and binding on the consumer.

The term "fuel" shall mean coal, oil and other forms of fuel used in boilers in the thermal power stations. The fuel cost variation adjustment shall be made on the basis of the combined average cost of fuel determined during the calendar month immediately preceding the month for which the bill is rendered.

13.14 Subsidies and Cross-Subsidisation

- **Low-income consumers and agriculture** often get subsidized rates.
- The burden is cross-subsidized by higher tariffs for commercial and industrial users.

Examples:

- **Tamil Nadu**: First 100 units free
- **Delhi**: 0 charges for ≤200 units
- **Punjab**: 300 free units for some households

Subsidies may be delivered directly via **Direct Benefit Transfer (DBT)** in pilot states.

13.15 Sample Tariff Comparison (100 Units Consumption)

State	Avg. Bill (₹)	Notes
Tamil Nadu	₹113	100 units free
Rajasthan	₹833	Higher base rates
Maharashtra	₹684–₹693	Rural rates slightly higher
Delhi	₹0 or ~₹400	Subsidized up to 400 units
Gujarat	₹325 (urban)	Efficient state-run DISCOMs
UP/Bihar/MP	₹600–₹700	High duties and base tariffs

13.16 Fuel Cost Adjustment (FCA) and Other Charges

Utilities revise bills quarterly to reflect rising/lowering cost of power procurement:

- **FCA**: Adjusts for changes in fuel cost
- **Electricity Duty**: Applied by states (percentage or per-unit basis)
- **Meter Rent/Service Fees**: Sometimes bundled into fixed charge

13.17 Industrial and Agricultural Tariffs

- **Industrial tariffs** may include load-based charges, ToD pricing, and power factor clauses.

- **Agriculture** may be flat-rate (e.g., ₹180/BHP/year in UP) or free (Punjab).

13.18 Legal and Policy Framework

Relevant laws:

- **Electricity Act 2003**: SERCs to determine tariffs

- **Electricity Rules 2020**: Billing transparency

- **National Tariff Policy**: Cost-reflective tariffs, reduction of cross-subsidy

13.19 The Physics of Electricity Tariffs: From Grid to Bill

Electricity tariffs are not merely administrative constructs or policy decisions — they are deeply rooted in the physical behaviour of electrical systems.

The bill a consumer receives is the end point of a chain of causation that begins with physics: energy is generated, transported through a network that imposes resistance and losses at every stage, transformed multiple times between voltage levels, and finally delivered to the consumer. Each step in this chain has a cost, and the sum of those costs — plus the capital investment in infrastructure, the cost of fuel, operation and maintenance, and the regulatory mandated return — determines what the tariff must recover. Understanding this chain is essential to understanding why tariffs are structured the way they are.

Modern tariff design increasingly follows the principle of cost causation: the entity that causes a cost should bear that cost. Different consumer categories cause very different costs. An industrial consumer with a stable, high-load-factor demand uses infrastructure efficiently and requires few voltage transformation stages; a residential consumer with spiky, low-load-factor demand causes higher peak investment and more distribution losses. These physical differences justify differentiated tariff structures, and they explain why the principle of cost-reflective tariffs — central to India's National Tariff Policy — requires moving away from politically determined flat rates toward prices that reflect actual system usage.

13.20 Technical and Commercial Losses as a Hidden Tax on Consumers

Transmission and distribution losses represent the gap between the energy injected into the system at the generation end and the energy actually billed to consumers. These losses are of two kinds. Technical losses arise from the physical properties of the network: resistance in conductors dissipates energy as heat (I^2R losses), transformer cores consume energy, and reactive power flows impose additional current without contributing usable power. Commercial losses arise from theft, defective metering, billing errors, and unauthorised connections.

Since utilities must recover the cost of all energy purchased or generated — including the portion lost — higher aggregate technical and commercial (AT&C) losses directly increase the tariff burden on paying consumers. In effect, theft and inefficiency in the system function as a hidden tax on honest consumers. India's national AT&C loss target under RDSS is 12–15%, and reductions in losses achieved through smart metering and network upgrades directly translate into lower average cost of supply, enabling more cost-reflective and equitable tariffs.

13.21 Peak Demand: Why You Pay for the Worst Fifteen Minutes

A fundamental characteristic of electricity is that it cannot be stored economically at grid scale. Generation must match demand at every instant. The electricity system must therefore be designed and built to meet peak demand — the maximum load that occurs at the most demanding moment — even if that peak is far above the average. When peak demand arrives, the most expensive generation sources (such as gas turbines or diesel generators held in reserve) are called upon, driving up the marginal cost of supply.

This is the physical reason for demand charges in industrial tariffs: the maximum demand recorded during a billing period (typically over a 15–30 minute interval) is used to determine the infrastructure that must be available for that consumer. A consumer who uses electricity unevenly — consuming heavily for short periods — imposes a larger infrastructure cost than a consumer who draws the same total energy steadily. The introduction of Time-of-Day (ToD) tariffs and smart meters in India reflects this reality: by pricing peak-hour consumption higher than off-peak consumption, tariffs signal the true cost of electricity at each moment and encourage consumers to shift flexible loads to lower-cost periods, improving overall system efficiency.

13.22 Fixed Costs and the Existence Charge: Paying for the Grid Even Without Using It

A significant portion of electricity supply costs are fixed: they are incurred regardless of how much electricity is actually consumed. Capital investment in power plants, transmission towers, transformers, substations, distribution lines, and meters must be recovered whether or not those assets are fully utilised. These fixed costs cannot be recovered solely through energy charges, because a consumer who uses very little electricity would pay almost nothing while still benefiting from the availability of the infrastructure. This is why tariffs include a fixed charge (also called a demand charge or standing charge) independent of consumption: it covers the cost of keeping the system connected and available.

The growing penetration of rooftop solar in India creates a new dimension to this issue. Consumers who install solar panels reduce their daytime purchases from the grid but continue to use the grid as a backup and for night-time supply. They therefore impose grid availability costs without contributing proportionately through energy charges. This has led regulators to revisit fixed charge structures and net metering policies, so that grid costs are equitably shared between solar and non-solar consumers rather than being shifted entirely onto those without rooftop installations.

13.23 Safety Infrastructure as a Tariff Component

Electricity tariffs implicitly include the cost of safety infrastructure, including insulation systems, earthing and grounding networks, surge arresters, protective relays, and circuit breakers throughout the distribution system. These investments reduce the risk of electric shock, equipment damage, fires, and service interruptions. They are not optional extras but mandatory elements of a compliant, safe electricity supply. Without them, faults cascade, outages become widespread, equipment is destroyed, and — critically — human lives are at risk.

Regulatory frameworks in the electricity sector extend beyond tariff determination to encompass safety enforcement, operational standards, and accident investigation. The Central Electricity Authority (CEA) in India sets technical standards for construction of electrical plants, lines, and metering — and these standards carry cost implications that are built into the tariff structure. Regulatory oversight ensures that utilities maintain safe and reliable systems, protecting both consumers and the long-term financial viability of the electricity sector. A well-maintained system with low accident rates also reduces insurance liabilities and emergency repair costs, contributing to system-wide cost efficiency over time.

13.24 Human Error, System Failures, and Their Financial Consequences

A significant proportion of electrical accidents and system failures arise not from equipment defects but from human error: improper switching, inadequate training, failure to follow lock-out/tag-out procedures before maintenance, and work on energised lines without adequate precautions. Beyond their safety consequences, these failures have direct financial implications. Equipment damaged by switching errors must be repaired or replaced. Outages caused by human error result in loss of billable energy. Regulatory penalties and compensation claims follow from failures to meet safety standards. And the reputational consequences of a serious accident can trigger costly regulatory investigations.

Training, skills certification, and procedural discipline in electricity operations are therefore not merely safety compliance requirements — they are cost management tools. Workforce competence directly reduces operational risk, lowers equipment damage rates, improves first-time fix rates during fault restoration, and shortens outage durations. In this sense, investment in human capital is as economically justified as investment in physical infrastructure, and its cost is legitimately part of the operation and maintenance component of the tariff.

13.25 Conclusion

Electricity tariffs in India are not uniform but reflect both policy intent and technical realities. While the two-part system supports efficient cost recovery, political pressures and consumer affordability lead to extensive subsidization. A rational tariff must balance consumer welfare, utility viability, and system efficiency, ideally backed by data-driven norms and regulatory transparency.

Chapter 14: Understanding Electricity Tariff Structures in India

In India, electricity tariffs for domestic consumers are determined by each State Electricity Regulatory Commission (SERC). Although most states follow similar principles, the exact rates and structures vary widely depending on local policies, subsidies, and cost structures.

14.1 Components of a Domestic Electricity Tariff

Most Indian states follow a two-part tariff system:

1. **Fixed Charge**: A flat fee independent of usage, meant to cover infrastructure and service costs. This may vary by consumer load type (single-phase or three-phase) or sanctioned load (e.g., ₹50–₹200/month).

2. **Energy Charge (Usage-Based)**: Billed per unit (kWh) consumed, typically using a **slab-wise**

telescopic system. The rate increases progressively with consumption:

Example:

- ₹2/kWh for first 50 units
- ₹4/kWh for 51–150 units
- ₹6/kWh for 151–300 units
- ₹8/kWh above 300 units

This protects low-volume consumers by ensuring the lowest rates apply to the first block of usage.

14.2 Sample Slab Billing Illustration

Consider a consumer using 250 units in two different states:

- **State A**: Fixed charge ₹100; slabs as above.
- **State B**: Fixed ₹50; energy charges ₹4/unit for 0–50 units, ₹6/unit for 51–200 units, ₹8/unit beyond that.

Bill Calculation for State A:

- ₹100 + (100×₹3) + (100×₹5) + (50×₹7) = ₹100 + ₹300 + ₹500 + ₹350 = ₹1,250

Bill for State B:

- ₹50 + (50×₹4) + (150×₹6) + (50×₹8) = ₹50 + ₹200 + ₹900 + ₹400 = ₹1,550

14.3 Subsidies and Cross-Subsidization

Many states subsidize low-income or low-usage consumers, with costs recovered from industrial/commercial users (cross-subsidization).

- **Tamil Nadu** offers the first 100 units free.
- **Delhi** provides full subsidy for usage ≤200 units and partial for 201–400 units.
- **Punjab** gives 300 free units to eligible households.

14.4 Electricity Duty, FCA, and Other Charges

Additional components often include:

- **Electricity Duty** (varies by state, as percentage or fixed per unit)
- **Fuel Cost Adjustment (FCA)**: Adjusts for generation cost changes quarterly

- **Meter Rent/Other Charges**: Usually included in fixed charge

14.5 Emerging Trends

- **Time-of-Day (ToD) Tariffs**: Some states like Uttarakhand are introducing variable pricing by time slot.
- **Smart Metering**: Enables real-time billing and ToD tariffs.

14.6 Comparison of Effective Costs for 100 Units (2023)

State	Avg. Cost (₹/100 units)	Notes
Tamil Nadu	₹113	100 units free policy
Rajasthan	₹833	High fixed charge, minimal subsidy
Maharashtra	₹684–₹693	Higher charges for rural areas
Delhi	₹0 or ~₹400	Subsidies up to 400 units

| Gujarat | ₹325 (urban) | Lower-cost state discoms |
| Bihar/UP/MP | ₹600–₹700+ | High base tariffs + electricity duties |

14.7 Conclusion

Electricity tariffs for households across India remain highly state-specific, reflecting regional policies and political priorities. While progressive slab systems protect small consumers, total billing is also affected by fixed charges, taxes, and subsidies. Understanding these elements is essential for reforming power distribution and ensuring affordable energy access.

Chapter 15: Privatisation of DISCOMs in India

India's power distribution sector has seen a growing trend towards privatisation, driven by high AT&C losses and poor service in some public DISCOMs. This chapter explores the rationale, models, and state-level progress of DISCOM reforms.

15.1 Models of Privatisation

- **Distribution Licensee (PPP) Model**: Private entity holds majority ownership of the DISCOM (e.g., Delhi, Odisha).
- **Franchisee Model**: Utility remains state-owned, but a private firm operates a specific area (e.g., Bhiwandi, Agra).

15.2 Notable Examples of Privatization

- **Delhi**: Privatised in 2002. AT&C losses dropped from 55% to under 10%. Tata and BSES operate distribution.
- **Odisha**: Tata Power now operates all four state DISCOMs under a PPP model (2020 onwards).
- **Bhiwandi (Maharashtra)**: Torrent Power reduced losses from 58% to 15%.
- **Agra (UP)**: Losses cut from 59% to 16% under franchisee model.

15.3 Recent Developments in Different States

- **Uttar Pradesh (2025)**: Tendered Dakshinanchal & Purvanchal DISCOMs for privatisation. Franchise model under consideration for Meerut, Varanasi.
- **Union Territories**: Dadra & Nagar Haveli, Daman & Diu privatised (Torrent Power). Chandigarh process ongoing.
- **Electricity (Amendment) Bill 2022**: Introduced in Lok Sabha in August 2022 and referred to the Standing Committee on Energy, this bill proposes significant reforms to the Electricity

Act 2003. Key provisions include: allowing multiple distribution licensees (DISCOMs) to operate in the same area on a non-discriminatory open access basis; mandating the fixing of minimum and maximum tariff ceilings by CERC and SERCs to prevent predatory pricing; prescribing a minimum Renewable Purchase Obligation (RPO) percentage by the Union government; strengthening payment security mechanisms; and establishing an Electricity Contract Enforcement Authority (ECEA) to handle contract-related disputes. The bill also proposes timely tariff revision by SERCs. As of early 2026, the bill remains under consideration by the Standing Committee. Several state governments have raised concerns about it encroaching on state powers over electricity, which is a concurrent subject under the Constitution.

15.4 State-wise Summary

State	Status	Notes
Delhi	Fully privatised	Tata Power/BSES operate

	(2002)	
Odisha	PPP with Tata Power	All DISCOMs under PPP since 2020
Maharashtra	Franchises (Bhiwandi, Nagpur)	MSEDCL remains public
UP	Privatisation tenders in 2025	Focus on high-loss DISCOMs
Karnataka	Public DISCOMs (BESCOM etc.)	Prefers internal reform, cautious on privatisation
Tamil Nadu	Fully public	Emphasis on subsidy-led reforms

15.5 Key Regulatory Reform: Electricity (Amendment) Rules 2022 – Rule 14 (Fuel and Power Purchase Cost Passthrough)

A major regulatory development that has significantly improved DISCOM finances was the amendment of Rule 14 of the Electricity Rules 2005, implemented in December 2022. This amendment mandated automatic monthly passthrough of fuel and power purchase cost adjustment surcharges to consumers, effectively depoliticising tariff revisions. Previously, DISCOMs had to wait for annual or multi-year tariff proceedings to recover increased fuel costs, leading to persistent revenue deficits. By making cost recovery automatic and monthly, this change removed a long-standing structural problem in DISCOM financial management. By FY 2024–25, 30 of India's 36 states and Union Territories had adopted regulations aligned with Rule 14. As a direct result, the gap between average cost of supply (ACS) and average revenue realised (ARR) — which measures DISCOM financial health — narrowed dramatically from 65 paise per unit in 2020–21 to just 6 paise per unit by FY 2024–25. Several DISCOMs that previously reported large losses returned to profitability by FY25. For example, MSEDCL (Maharashtra) reported a profit of ₹508 crore in FY25, compared to a ₹5,000 crore loss the previous year. Similarly, the Late Payment Surcharge (LPS) Rules, which penalise DISCOMs for delayed payments to generators, have improved payment discipline across the sector.

15.6 Revamped Distribution Sector Scheme (RDSS)

The Revamped Distribution Sector Scheme (RDSS), launched in 2021–22, is a reform-based and results-linked government scheme with a total financial outlay of ₹3.03 lakh crore over five years (ending March 2026). Its primary objectives are to: (a) reduce aggregate technical and commercial (AT&C) losses to 12–15% at the national level; (b) close the gap between average cost of supply and average revenue realised (ACS-ARR gap) to zero by FY25; and (c) deploy 250 million smart prepaid consumer meters. RDSS provides financial assistance to DISCOMs for infrastructure upgrades, subject to pre-qualifying criteria and achievement of minimum benchmarks. Under RDSS, states must ensure timely payment of government department dues, subsidy release, and payment discipline to generating companies. The scheme also funds upgrades to distribution infrastructure including feeder separation, transformer metering, and modernisation of substations. The national AT&C loss has reduced to around 15.37% by FY25 as a result of combined RDSS implementation and smart meter deployment. As of 2024, RDSS has sanctioned installation of nearly 20 million smart meters and replacement of inefficient streetlights with LED lights. States such as Bihar and Uttar Pradesh have made notable progress in smart meter installation under RDSS, though nationwide deployment speed needs further acceleration to meet the 250 million target within the scheme period.

15.7 Conclusion

Privatisation is not one-size-fits-all. While Delhi and Odisha show successful transitions, other states prefer selective outsourcing or public sector reforms. The future may see more competition, not just privatisation, especially if amendments enabling multiple licensees pass. The performance of current models—franchisee or PPP—will shape further reforms across India.

Chapter 16: Smart Grid and Digital Metering

In recent years, the power sector in India has seen significant transformations with the advent of smart grid technologies and digital metering systems. These technologies aim to improve the efficiency, reliability, and sustainability of electricity supply and consumption.

16.1 What is a Smart Grid?

A smart grid is an advanced electricity network that integrates digital communication, control systems, and automation with the traditional power grid. It enables a two-way flow of electricity and information, allowing utilities and consumers to monitor and manage electricity usage in real-time.

Key features of a smart grid include:

- Real-time monitoring and control of grid operations

- Integration of renewable energy sources
- Automated outage detection and restoration
- Demand response and energy efficiency
- Enhanced cybersecurity and data analytics

16.2 Advanced Metering Infrastructure (AMI)

AMI refers to systems that measure, collect, and analyse energy usage, and communicate with metering devices such as smart meters. These meters provide real-time data to both utilities and consumers.

Advantages of AMI:

- Remote reading of electricity meters
- Elimination of manual meter reading errors
- Detection of electricity theft or tampering
- Time-of-day (ToD) or dynamic pricing
- Greater consumer awareness of energy usage

16.3 Prepaid and Smart Meters in India

The Government of India has been promoting the installation of smart and prepaid meters under various schemes, such as the Revamped Distribution Sector Scheme (RDSS).

Benefits of prepaid meters include:

- Upfront payment for electricity usage
- Reduced billing disputes
- Improved revenue collection for DISCOMs

India has been making significant progress in smart meter deployment under the Revamped Distribution Sector Scheme (RDSS). Smart meter installations accelerated sharply, rising from around 4,000 per day in 2022–23 to over 1,15,000 per day by May 2025, bringing the total deployed to over 31 million meters. The RDSS, with a total outlay of ₹3.03 lakh crore over five years, has sanctioned consumer meter installations across 22 crore connections. As of 2025, states including Uttar Pradesh, Bihar, Maharashtra, and Rajasthan have been leading in deployments, though a significant portion of the 250 million target remains to be installed. A key benefit of RDSS-linked meter deployment has been the improvement in billing and collection efficiency: by FY 2024–25, 21 utilities crossed the Ministry of Power's billing efficiency threshold of 92%, and 17 reported collection efficiency of 100%.

16.4 Challenges and Way Forward

Some challenges in smart grid adoption include:

- High initial cost of infrastructure
- Need for skilled manpower
- Ensuring cybersecurity of data

However, with policy support and ongoing reforms, smart grids and digital metering are expected to become the backbone of future electricity distribution in India.

Chapter 17: Sustainability and Renewable Integration

With the growing concern for climate change and energy security, the integration of renewable energy sources into the electricity grid has become a national priority.

17.1 India's Renewable Energy Targets

India has set ambitious renewable energy targets under its National Solar Mission and Nationally Determined Contributions (NDCs). The target is to achieve 500 GW of non-fossil fuel capacity by 2030. In a landmark achievement, India crossed 50% of its installed electricity capacity from non-fossil fuel sources in June 2025 — five years ahead of the NDC target. Total renewable energy installed capacity reached 253.96 GW by November 2025, an increase of over 23% compared to November 2024. India ranks 3rd globally in solar power installed capacity, 4th in wind power, and 4th in total renewable energy capacity (as per

IRENA RE Statistics 2025). In calendar year 2025 alone (up to November), India added 44.51 GW of renewable energy — nearly double the 24.72 GW added during the same period in 2024. Solar energy crossed 100 GW installed capacity in January 2025, reaching 132.85 GW by November 2025.

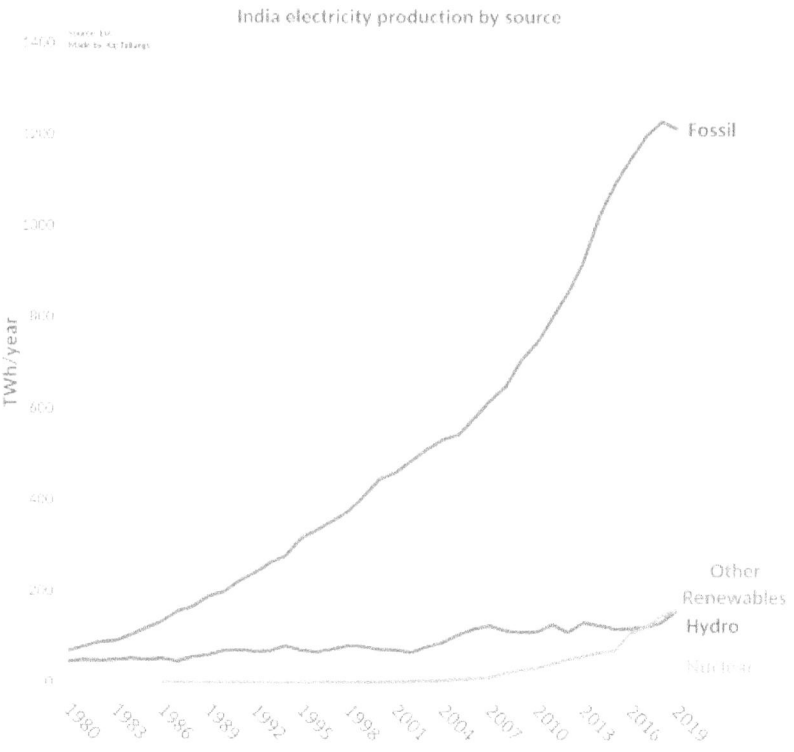

Figure: India's electricity production by source. By Kaj Tallungs - Own work, CC BY-SA 4.0, https://commons.wikimedia.org/w/index.php?curid=103211189

17.2 Grid Integration Challenges

Integration of renewable sources such as solar and wind into the grid presents several challenges:

- Variability and intermittency of generation
- Need for flexible generation sources or storage
- Transmission infrastructure in remote locations

Solutions include:

- Use of battery storage and pumped hydro storage
- Forecasting of renewable generation
- Development of Green Energy Corridors for transmission

17.3 Role of DISCOMs and Regulatory Commissions

DISCOMs and regulators are promoting:

- Net metering and rooftop solar adoption
- Time-of-day tariffs to shift consumption
- Renewable Purchase Obligations (RPOs) for obligated entities

17.4 Green Hydrogen and Future Technologies

Emerging technologies such as green hydrogen production using renewable electricity, floating solar, offshore wind, and agrivoltaics are being explored for the future.

India has launched the National Green Hydrogen Mission (NGHM) in January 2023, with a financial outlay of ₹19,744 crore up to 2029–30. The mission aims to produce 5 million metric tonnes of green hydrogen annually and install 60–100 GW of electrolyser capacity by 2030, positioning India as a global leader in green hydrogen production and export. As of 2025, the government has approved 4,12,000 tonnes per annum (TPA) of green hydrogen production and 3 GW of electrolyser capacity. Green hydrogen is seen as a critical decarbonisation tool for hard-to-abate sectors such as steel, fertiliser, and heavy transport.

17.5 PM Surya Ghar: Muft Bijli Yojana and PM-KUSUM

Two major government schemes have been instrumental in expanding rooftop and distributed solar energy in India. PM Surya Ghar: Muft Bijli Yojana (PMSG: MBY), launched in February 2024, aims to install rooftop solar systems in one crore (10 million) households across India, with a total outlay of ₹75,021 crore. Under the scheme, eligible residential consumers can get solar rooftop systems installed and receive free electricity for the units generated. From January 2025 to December 2025, nearly 14.43 lakh rooftop solar systems were installed across the country, benefiting over 18.14 lakh households. The government aims to add 30 GW of solar capacity through rooftop solar in the residential sector under this scheme, which is expected to generate 1 lakh crore units over 25 years and reduce 720 million metric tonnes of CO_2 emissions. Pradhan Mantri Kisan Urja Suraksha evam Utthaan Mahabhiyan (PM-KUSUM) scheme supports installation of solar pumps and solar power plants for farmers, helping reduce agricultural electricity subsidy burden on state DISCOMs and providing additional income to farmers. As of November 2025, 667.31 MW of solar power capacity has been installed under

Component-A of PM-KUSUM. These schemes are part of India's broader strategy to democratise renewable energy access and reduce the dependence of rural and agricultural consumers on the grid.

17.6 Conclusion

Renewable integration and sustainability are crucial for long-term energy security. With technological innovation, policy support, and investment, India is making steady progress towards a cleaner electricity future.

Chapter 18: Future Trends and Emerging Policies

This chapter outlines some future trends and policies shaping the Indian electricity sector in the coming decades.

18.1 Privatization of DISCOMs

Many states are initiating reforms to privatize distribution companies to improve efficiency and reduce losses. This includes:

- Franchising models
- Public-private partnerships (PPPs)
- Greater autonomy and accountability

18.2 One Nation, One Grid

This initiative aims to create a unified national electricity market through seamless interconnection of regional grids. It supports:

- Optimal power dispatch
- Reduction of power imbalances
- Improved grid stability

18.3 Direct Benefit Transfer (DBT) of Electricity Subsidy

To ensure targeted subsidy and reduce misuse, DBT is being piloted in states like Chandigarh and Dadra & Nagar Haveli. Under this system, subsidies are credited directly to the consumer's account.

18.4 Time-of-Day (ToD) Tariff and Smart Pricing

ToD tariffs charge different rates for electricity at different times of day, encouraging consumers to shift usage to off-peak hours. Smart meters make implementation feasible.

18.5 Role of AI and Automation

AI and machine learning are being used in:

- Load forecasting
- Predictive maintenance
- Theft detection
- Consumer usage profiling

18.6 Battery Energy Storage Systems (BESS) and Grid Stability

As India's share of intermittent renewable energy (solar and wind) increases, large-scale energy storage has become essential for grid stability. Battery Energy Storage Systems (BESS) store surplus renewable electricity during periods of high generation (such as daytime solar) and discharge it during periods of high demand or low generation. The Government of India approved a Viability Gap Funding (VGF) scheme for BESS development in September 2023, with a budget of ₹3,760 crore for implementation of 13.22 GWh of BESS capacity. In June 2025, an additional VGF scheme was approved for 30 GWh of BESS capacity with ₹5,400 crore support from the Power System Development Fund (PSDF). Alongside BESS, India is also investing in Pumped Storage Projects (PSPs) — a more mature form of grid-scale storage using water reservoirs. As of 2025, ten PSPs totalling 11,870 MW are under construction in the country. The National Electricity Plan (2023–2032) envisages expansion of the transmission network to 6.48 lakh circuit kilometres by 2032 (a 32% increase) and approval of 50.9 GW of inter-state transmission capacity to connect 280 GW of variable renewable energy by 2030. Offshore wind development is also being promoted, with the government offering VGF for the first 1 GW of offshore wind capacity. These storage and transmission investments are critical to enabling India's renewable energy ambitions without compromising grid reliability.

18.7 Conclusion

The future of electricity in India will be shaped by digitalization, decentralization, and decarbonization. Policymakers, utilities, and consumers must adapt to these shifts for a more resilient and efficient power sector.

Chapter 19: Conclusion

India's electricity sector has evolved remarkably over the past century, transitioning from localized supply systems during the British era to a vast, interconnected national grid governed by an elaborate regulatory and policy framework. This book has attempted to present a holistic and introductory overview of both the technical and legal dimensions of electricity supply and regulation in India.

In the first part of the book, we explored the technical aspects of electricity generation, transmission, distribution, metering, and protective systems. We looked into various sources of energy, from traditional coal and hydro to emerging renewable and smart grid technologies. Through chapters on substations, protective devices, and smart metering, we established a basic understanding of how power physically reaches our homes and industries.

The second part of the book focused on the legislative and regulatory framework that governs the sector. We traced the history of electricity legislation in India leading up to the Electricity Act of 2003, which brought significant liberalization and structural changes. We also studied the role of regulatory commissions, the national tariff policy, and the legal provisions that guide transmission, distribution, and trading of electricity.

Further, we examined electricity tariffs in depth—including how they are structured, the engineering principles (such as load factor and diversity), policy considerations, state-level variations, and efforts toward rationalization and subsidy management. We have also covered new developments such as DISCOM privatisation, smart meters, sustainability goals, renewable integration, and future trends like AI-driven load management, direct benefit transfer (DBT) of subsidies, and 'One Nation One Grid'.

While India has made significant strides in increasing generation capacity and improving electrification rates, the sector still faces challenges such as AT&C losses, financial stress on DISCOMs, inefficient tariff structures, and resistance to reform in some states. Nevertheless, with policy support, technology adoption, and regulatory discipline, India is poised to create a resilient, efficient, and consumer-friendly power sector.

It is hoped that this book provides a useful starting point for students, policy observers, professionals, and the curious reader to understand the critical elements of electricity supply and regulation in India. As reforms deepen and technologies evolve, staying updated and engaged with this dynamic field becomes all the more important.

Let us move forward with a commitment to energy equity, sustainability, and smart governance—for a brighter, well-powered India.

About the Author

Siva Prasad Bose is an author of various introductory guidebooks related to aspects of Indian laws. He is retired after over 30 years of service in Uttar Pradesh Power Corporation Limited in Lucknow. He received his electrical engineering degree from Jadavpur University, Kolkata and has a law degree from Meerut University, Meerut and a BSc from MMH College Ghaziabad. His interests lie in the fields of family law, civil law, law of contracts, and areas of law related to power electricity related issues.

Other Books by Siva Prasad Bose

Introduction to Wills and Probate

Senior Citizens Abuse in India

Introduction to Negotiable Instruments

Introduction to Marriage Laws in India

Neighbour Problems in India and what to do about them

Managing Court Cases with Mental Strength

Delays in Court Cases in India

Self-Publish Books and E-Books in India

Introduction to Patents and Patent Law in India

Introduction to Property Law in India

www.ingramcontent.com/pod-product-compliance
Lightning Source LLC
Chambersburg PA
CBHW052357220526
45465CB00003BB/1143